ALSO BY J. D. McCLATCHY

POETRY

Scenes from Another Life | *1981*
Stars Principal | *1986*
The Rest of the Way | *1990*
Ten Commandments | *1998*
Hazmat | *2002*
Division of Spoils | *2003*
Mercury Dressing | *2011*

ESSAYS

White Paper | *1989*
Twenty Questions | *1998*
American Writers at Home | *2004*

AS EDITOR

Anne Sexton: The Poet and Her Critics | *1978*
Recitative: Prose by James Merrill | *1986*
Poets on Painters | *1988*
The Vintage Book of Contemporary American Poetry | *1990, 2003*
Woman in White: Poems by Emily Dickinson | *1991*
The Vintage Book of Contemporary World Poetry | *1996*

Christmas Poems (with John Hollander) | *1999*

Longfellow: Poems and Other Writings | *2000*

On Wings of Song | *2000*

Love Speaks Its Name | *2001*

Poems of the Sea | *2001*

Bright Pages: Yale Writers, 1701–2001 | *2001*

Horace: The Odes | *2002*

Edna St. Vincent Millay: Selected Poems | *2003*

Poets of the Civil War | *2005*

Thornton Wilder: Collected Plays & Writings on Theater | *2007*

*The Whole Difference: Selected Writings of Hugo von
    Hofmannsthal* | *2008*

The Four Seasons | *2008*

*Thornton Wilder: The Bridge of San Luis Rey and Other Novels
    1926–1948* | *2009*

Anthony Hecht: Selected Poems | *2011*

*Thornton Wilder: The Eighth Day, Theophilus North,
    Autobiographical Writings* | *2011*

W. S. Merwin: Collected Poems | *2013*

(WITH STEPHEN YENSER)

James Merrill: Collected Poems | *2001*

James Merrill: Collected Novels and Plays | *2002*

James Merrill: Collected Prose | *2004*

James Merrill: The Changing Light at Sandover | *2006*

James Merrill: Selected Poems | *2008*

AS TRANSLATOR

The Magic Flute | *2000, 2006*

Carmen | *2001*

Seven Mozart Librettos | *2010*

The Bartered Bride | *2011*

The Barber of Seville | *2012*

PLUNDERED HEARTS

PLUNDERED HEARTS

NEW AND SELECTED POEMS

J. D. McCLATCHY

 ALFRED A. KNOPF · NEW YORK · 2014

THIS IS A BORZOI BOOK
PUBLISHED BY ALFRED A. KNOPF

Copyright © 2014 by J. D. McClatchy

All rights reserved under International and Pan-American
Copyright Conventions. Published in the United States by Alfred A. Knopf,
a division of Random House LLC, New York, and simultaneously
in Canada by Random House of Canada Limited, Toronto,
Penguin Random House companies.

www.aaknopf.com/poetry

Knopf, Borzoi Books, and the colophon are
registered trademarks of Random House LLC.

Library of Congress Cataloging-in-Publication Data
McClatchy, J. D., 1945–
    [Poems. Selections]
    Plundered Hearts : New and Selected Poems / By J. D. McClatchy.
    —First Edition.
        pages cm
    "Distributed by Random House, Inc., New York."
    ISBN 978-0-385-35151-5 (Hardcover)—ISBN 978-0-385-35152-2 (eBook)
    I. Title.
    PS3563.A26123A6   2014
    811'.54—dc23   2013023979

Jacket painting: *Sleep* by Vincent Desiderio, 2008. Image courtesy of
Marlborough Gallery.
Jacket design by Chip Kidd

Manufactured in the United States of America
First Edition

for Chip Kidd

CONTENTS

from Mercury Dressing | 2009

NEW POEMS

MY HAND COLLECTION

Arranged around the lamp's mercury glass globe,
    They reach out for or defend against
The attention that wood or bronze or resin
    Shakily command at this late stage
Of reproduction. After all, none is like
    My own one of a kind, its rigging
Of creases, its scuffed half-moons and bitten nails,
    Its quivering index and moiré
Pattern of skin loosely draped over the bones—
    Liver spots carelessly spilled on it,
Along with whatever dings or oily stains
    The insincere handshake and backslap,
The dog's tongue or jock's package have left behind.
    Those on this table are innocent.
The pair unscrewed from a side chapel's martyr
    Still holding crazed flakes of their own thumbs,
The pharaoh's fist implacably denying
    The idea there are more gods than one,
A factory glove mold, the madam's ring holder,
    A mannequin's milk-white come-hither,
The miniature ecstatic's stigmata,
    Someone's smartly cuffed, celluloid brooch,
A Buddha's gilded fingertips joined and poised,
    Like a conductor's, at last to re-
lease the final, tremulous, resolving chord—
    Each frozen in a single gesture,
Pleading, threatening, clinging, shielding, the sorry
    Travelling company called Fierce Desire,
These here on the left knowing only too well
    What those on the right have been up to.
Patiently assembled on their glass senate
    Floor, forever in session, the *ayes*

Have it over and over again (despite
　　Gloria Vanderbilt's birthday gift,
A rough-cut back-country tobaccoed pine paw
　　That flatly refuses to take sides).

And of living hands, how many have I held,
　　As it were, for keeps—say, wordlessly,
After the promise that bodies can make, held
　　While staring at his sweetly shut eyes.
What, time and again, was I holding onto,
　　As if it had been for dear life's sake?
Looking back, I guess I am glad they let go.
　　Theirs are not the hands that haunt me now.
The one that does belonged to a blustery,
　　Timid soul at home in dull routines,
Forfeiting glamour and curiosity,
　　A life sustained by its denials.
I reached for it, only because B-movies
　　Demand one pick it up off the sheet,
A shrivelled, damp, and fetid wedge still clutching
　　Nothing but a bed railing of air,
Its slackened tendons stiff and crusted with scabs
　　And knots of scar tissue abutting
Deep-sunk hematomas, from which the knucklebones
　　Jutted like cairns, nails cracked and yellow.
Though dead for hours, it was not yet cold.
　　I didn't know what to do with it.
So I held onto it without wanting to,
　　Fearful of letting it go too soon.
It was what—now for the last time—I *first* held.
　　It was a hand. It was my mother's.

THREE POEMS BY WILHELM MÜLLER

1. On the Stream

How swift you rushed along,
Your torrent so wild, so bright.
How quiet you have become.
No farewell words tonight.

A hard, unyielding crust
Hides you where you stand.
Cold and motionless you lie
There, on your bed of sand.

On your surface I scratch
With a sharp stone's edge
The name of my beloved,
The day, the hour, the pledge:

The day when first we met,
The day I left in spring,
Name and numbers inside
The shape of a broken ring.

And in this brook, my heart,
Do you see yourself portrayed?
See beneath its frozen crust
The turbulent cascade?

2. The Gray Head

The frost had left a white
Covering on my head.
I thought I had grown old.
At last! I joyfully said.

It melted soon enough.
Again my hair was black.
I am left here with my youth.
The grave I seek draws back.

Between the dusk and dawnlight
Many heads turned gray.
Imagine! Mine has not,
Having come now all this way.

3. The Hurdy-Gurdy Man

There, beyond the village,
Stands a hurdy-gurdy man.
His fingers numb with cold,
He plays as best he can.

Barefoot on the ice,
To and fro he sways.
The little plate beside him
Is empty day after day.

No one stops to listen,
Or even notice him.
The dogs start to snarl
When the old man begins.

And he lets it all go by,
Lets it go as it will.
He grinds the wooden handle,
His hand is never still.

O wondrous old man,
Will you take me along?
Will your hurdy-gurdy
Ever play my song?

PRELUDE, DELAY, AND EPITAPH

1.

A finger is cut from a rubber glove
And cinched as a tourniquet around my toe.
The gouging ingrown nail is to be removed.
The shots supposed to have pricked and burned
The nerves diabetes has numbed never notice.
The toe, as I watch, slowly turns a bluish
Gray, the color of flesh on a slab, the size
Of a fetus floating on the toilet's Styx,
But lumpen, the blunt hull of a tug slowly
Nosing the huge, clumsy vessel into port.

2.

The February
Moon, its arms around itself,
Still sits stalled beneath

Points being made about love
And death in the sky above.

The moral is spread
On some month-old snow out back—
A design we like

To think night can make of day,
The summons again delayed.

3.

You who read this too will die.
None loved his life as much as I,
Yet trees burst brightly into bloom
Without me, here in my darkened room.

THE NOVELIST

The books sit silently on the shelf,
Their spines broken but unresentful.
He sits there too, thinking to himself
Of nothing—at last an uneventful
Evening, an hour to sulk or drift,
No joy to worry, no burden to lift,

As if on board some two-star ocean
Liner, able to roam at will
While confined to its slow motion
Through the middle of nowhere until
The dinner bell when the stateroom saves
Him from what he both avoids and craves.

Company. Others. The idle crowd
Beyond his bolted metal door—
So insatiable, so empty and loud.
Then, for a moment, the corridor
Seems like a page in some *roman-fleuve*
Where people live the lives they deserve.

A young man arrives in the glittering city.
The heroine writes her famous letter.
Emma stares at the vial with pity.
Pierre or Pip promises to do better.
Men and women find in each other
Why he must kill rather than love her.

In other words, it resembles the world
In the books above him, where so much
Sadness is fingered and then unfurled.
The wrong address, the inadvertent touch,
The revolution, the unanswered call,
The poisoned bouquet, the back-alley brawl.

He changes his mind. He will accept
The captain's invitation to dine.
His secret, after all, can be kept
Like those on the shelf: chance and design,
Until opened, closed but in reach,
Like words before they become speech.

ONE YEAR LATER

In this photograph
He is knee-deep in water,
Half-smiling, half-scared.

His cracked Transformer,
His knapsack, his cup, his cat.
Why did they survive?

How is it we leave so much
Behind for others to touch?

.

Ministers, tell me,
Why did you think that power
Would stay where it was?

Aging cores collapse
Under waves of a future
No one can live in.

The reactors stand there still.
What is left to warm or kill?

.

The news crawl's moved on
To other smaller, larger,
Distant disasters.

Get on with your life,
A shy inner voice insists
On the crowded screen.

Our lives lengthen into death,
As if into one last breath.

•

He watched for too long.
He could not run fast enough.
He was lifted up

With all the others
Into reruns of the day
No one's come back from.

When I took that photograph
He was seven and a half.

March 11, 2012

WOLF'S TREES

If trees fall in a wood and no one hears them,
Do they exist except as a page of lines
That words of rapture or grief are written on?
They are lines too while alive, pointing away
From the primer of damped air and leafmold
That underlie, or would if certain of them
Were not melon or maize, solferino or smoke,
Colors into which a sunset will collapse
On a high branch of broken promises.
Or they nail the late summer's shingles of noon
Back onto the horizon's overlap, reflecting
An emptiness visible on leaves that come and go.

How does a life flash before one's eyes
At the end? How is there time for so much time?
You pick up the book and hold it, knowing
Long since the failed romance, the strained
Marriage, the messenger, the mistake,
Knowing it all at once, as if looking through
A lighted dormer on the dark crest of a barn.
You know who is inside, and who has always been
At the other edge of the wood. She is waiting
For no one in particular. It could be you.
If you can discover which tree she has become,
You will know whether it has all been true.

for Wolf Kahn

BACON'S EASEL

On it, the figure of something dead
Inside a man who's penetrated
Another man articulated
Against a square that could be read

As a proper balance or a purple bruise.
They go about it silently,
Neither rapt, neither free
To do as he might elsewhere choose.

The one, his head wrenched to the side,
His scrotum like a cortex but hairy,
His penis eerily catenary,
Seems to know the other has lied.

The other *has* lied, pretending
To like a no-questions-asked
Approach to love's brutal task
And the overmastered scream it ends in.

.

Around it, tiny continents
Of rust on the lids of oil paint,
Brushes in coffee tins, the faint
Smell of urine and arguments.

Propped up are the photographs
Of martyrs and their rigmarole,
The open car and grassy knoll,
A wartime starlet's shimmery calf,

And clippings from some local paper,
The story of a boy who'd seen
His father shove a rifle between
His silent mother's legs and rape her.

He sat on a folding stool and stared
At what he'd done. The edges of flesh
Where the colors unpredictably thresh—
There is the soul's final repair.

PALM BEACH SIGHTINGS

The topiaried ficus shrub,
Snipped into monumentality,
Can neither slump its shoulders nor shrug
When its pyramid complains, "Why me?"

•

Raucous parakeets
In the crotch of a palm stump
Find their tax haven.

•

The supermarket's valet parker,
Who lives with a storied widow rent-free,
Sites his orange cone to earmark her
Slip of shade for the silver Bentley—
The color her hair would be were it not
For the bi-stylist who'd asked her to fox-trot.

•

For the dog wedding,
I brought matching jeweled leashes,
Modelled on my own.

•

From the scarab bracelet of boutiques on Worth
Dangle offices, discrete but palatial,
For jowls that look like an afterbirth
Before the peel and stem-cell facial.

KISS KISS

The opera prompter makes a kissing sound—
Backstage bunkum now signaling dismay—
To force the off-key tenor to turn around
And follow her hand toward the requisite A.

.

At the singer's subsequent biopsy,
The stolid doctor's puckered lips
Mimic the site the slickened tube
Enters and leaves with a faint smack,
While overhead the Blue Danube
Stutters on a damaged track.

MY ROBOTIC PROSTATECTOMY

The surgeon sat at his desk in a niche
On the far side of the OR,
Ready to power up the robot
I lay facing, its arms still shrouded
In plastic as if just delivered
From the dry cleaners. My mask
Was snapped on, the drip unclamped.
That was the last I saw of this iron man

Whom a computer's knobs directed
To motivate the forceps breaching
The tissue walls so elfin scissors
Could do what it once took three hags
To manage—hold, measure, and cut
The thread that would tie off the lemon-
Large defect planning in time
To bring the whole contraption down.

So what did they cut out of me?
My past? The source of the little death
Clenched at the climax of one
Of the few unambiguous pleasures
And now, slowly or suddenly, riddled
With a cancer only mildly threatening
But still urgently reminding me of how,
The older one gets, the past matters

Less and less. What's wanted now,
I realize, is not my old life
Back again, but anyone's life—
Yours, say, so long as it lasts.
If only a course of radiation

Next could scorch the still remaining
Traces of what is killing me—
Metastasizing nostalgia.

Oh, what did they cut out of me?
A future? I had imagined it as a shaded
Chaise near the pool, but will find myself
Shuffling in diapers, chapped and snappish,
Down its corridor, meanly overconfident,
Bored at having joined the ranks
Of beribboned Survivors who never stop
Nattering on about their close calls.

When I check out, the receptionist
Reviews the charges and happens on
The overlooked pathologist's
Report, and running her finger down
The rows of obscure acronyms
And variable percentages
To the bottom line, she looks up
Past my credit card, clucking

With good news: *the borders are clear.*
It is as if a mist has lifted
And he stands there on the other side,
The other iron man, not impatient
But, yes, more obvious than before,
Knowing that sooner or later I must,
Though the terms and timing are unknown,
Step forward at last to meet him, alone.

TWO ARIAS FROM *THE MARRIAGE OF FIGARO*

1. Non più andrai

No more now will you flutter by
To bother the ladies night and day,
You preening, lovesick butterfly!
Let those beauties enjoy their rest.
No more now the ruffles and frills,
That feathered hat, all flash and flare,
That wavy hair, that dashing air,
Those cheeks so pink and caressed.
Off to the wars, my young friend!
Long mustaches and socks to mend,
Musket to shoulder, saber in place,
Back like a ramrod, sneer on your face,
A helmet to wear, my fine legionnaire,
Honor to squander, not a cent to spare.
No fancy balls and minuets,
Now it's all marching and bayonets.
Mountains, marshes, one by one,
Chilled by snow, scorched by sun.
How shrill the bugle call,
How loud the cannonball,
Blunderbuss and caterwaul,
All muddy, bitter, and gory.
On to victory, Cherubino!
Here's to military glory!

2. *Dove sono*

Where are they now, the vanished days,
The moments of pleasure's afterglow?
Where are the vows, the murmured praise
Spoken by that liar so long ago?

Why, if sweetness turns to regret,
If every hope becomes a grief,
Why is it still I cannot forget
The love that vies with disbelief?

If only my waiting, my long endurance,
The patience that true love imparts,
Could bring the slightest reassurance
Of changing his ungrateful heart!

HIS OWN LIFE

Who scorns his own life is lord of yours.

—SENECA

The morning sunlight on the window ledge
Was the signal he should start to kill himself.
Weeks before, it had been carefully planned.
The pills were lined up on the tray beside his bed
In tiny piles so he could swallow ten at a time,
White oblongs ridged across the middle
Like a trench between Help and Helplessness.
It had been so long now and, a doctor himself,
He knew what more he would have to endure
Before the body had worn itself out.
The suppurating pustules were multiplying
In his anus that drooled or spewed out gouts
Of acid-hot blood, the trail of which
He saw from the john he could never reach in time.

Time. What had once been flashed on a screen
As a sequence of familiar shots from a past
No one else would understand—the father's slap,
The sister's moonlit breasts, the teacher's pen,
The lover's mole, the inch of vintage mescal—
The carousel of slides we call a lifetime
I suppose went through his head, but how could I know?
It is as likely nothing was there, the mind stunned
And drifting from blurred maples in a square
To a painful wrinkle in the sheet beneath his thigh.
It was time. It was the plan. But it was hard to move.
He reached for the pills, pushing his hand deeper
Into the sun's warmth, which quickly overtook
His arm, his neck, his face, until he surrendered.

23

When, embracing her, he seemed to hesitate,
His wife pleaded not to witness his courage
But to share it. He relented. They both opened their wrists
With his sword. Because of his frailty, his blood ran
Too slowly, so he cut the veins in his ankles and knees,
Then looked up, fearful he would lose his purpose
If his wife were forced to stare at his torment.
He sent her away and summoned several scribes,
Sitting on the cold marble steps and dictating
Maxims still quoted today by those who think
They know how they would want to live a last day.
But death would not come. He asked a friend
To prepare the same poison used to execute
Those Athenian trials had condemned, and drank it down.

It was dark. It was the agreed-upon hour.
I had the key and quietly let myself in.
A lamp had been left on in the corridor.
I walked through its precaution toward the bedroom.
This is what we had decided, the dead man,
His lover, and I. I would "discover" the body.
The lover would pointedly—bantering with the doorman—
Arrive a half-hour later. Then, together,
We would call the police and, in one frantic
And one somber voice, report an apparent suicide.
The bedroom was dark, but I could see the body,
On the bed, under a sheet, its profile gaunt.
I turned the overhead light on and knew at once
Something was wrong. The face should be paler.

I went to it and screamed his name. Twice.
I heard the faintest groan. An eyelid moved.
There were too many pills still on the tray. Again
I called his name. I put my fingers on his neck,

But could feel nothing, hear nothing. I knew,
Though, that he was alive. I sat on the bed
Beside him and stared. Enough time passed
For shock not to have noticed. The doorbell rang.
What would I tell my friend now? What would we do?
I followed my crumbs of dread back to the door,
And opened it with the latch on, though expecting
The very person who was anxiously standing there.
I let him in, and could think of nothing but the truth.
"He's still alive." Eyes rolling back, he collapsed.

In a city where tyrants kill their mothers and children,
Why would they not soon turn against their teachers?
We may decide how but never precisely when
We leave. His barely clothed body was so cold
It stalled the poison's effect. Silently,
They waited. Organizing a death as drama
Had proved too difficult, the tableau disarranged
By the mind's eye in conflict with the body's
Stubborn clutch at life, its blind refusal.
So what he thought would be was behind him now.
What good was sentiment or ideas? You shape,
When you can, the middle of things—where in fact
The story begins—not the beginning or the end.
He asked his slaves to carry him to the steam room.

Meanwhile, we sat in the living room, debating what
To think, to feel, to do. We decided the sun
Was to blame, its warmth sapping the will,
Lulling the dying man's resolve, ruining the plan
He had weeks ago listened to abstractly,
Wanting and not wanting what he nodded to.
We spoke as if he were not in the next room.
We had three options. We could—this would be the one

He wanted—hold a pillow over his face
And do what he was finally unable to for himself.
Or we could leave and return the next day, hopeful
By then his weakness had solved the situation.
But there were witnesses that we were here now
And an autopsy would finger us as accomplices.

The third choice was inhuman but morally right.
Since I could not kill a man, even one I wanted dead,
And because I did not want to end up a criminal,
We called 911 and asked for an ambulance—
What our friend had begged to avoid, the Emergency
Room's brutal vanities. Within minutes they had arrived
In battle gear, quickly guessed the truth,
Strapped the victim to the gurney and, with genuine
Deference, told us everything would be done
To see that it was a quick and painless death.
A silent ride to the hospital in the crowded back.
We sat at the foot of his bed as he was examined.
A nurse told everyone to wait in the hallway.
She drew a curtain and stayed inside with him.

First, he is lowered into a pool of hot water.
How long does it take to die? a young man asks.
A lifetime, the philosopher replies with a smile.
He hopes the water will speed both the blood
And the hemlock. When he sees the water darken,
He weakly takes a handful and sprinkles the slaves,
A libation to Jupiter the Liberator.
Let us continue our journey, he bids them next,
And they carry him at last to the steam room,
Where, choking, he is soon suffocated.
His will, written while he was still powerful,
Specified his ashes be buried with no ceremony.

He would allow no one to praise or flatter him
For merely having anticipated his own death.

The doctor stood before us with a look
Whose pursed lips and downcast eyes
Spelled trouble. There had been a complication.
The nurse who had taken charge is a Catholic.
She says she sat with your friend for about an hour,
Then whispered to him, Do you want to live?
There was no response at first, but then she says
He said, Yes. Again she asked. Yes.
She reported it, leaving me no choice
But to do everything we can to keep him alive.
I know this is clearly not what anyone wants
But you must realize our legal jeopardy.
So a ventilator, mask, and tubes were brought.
Our comatose friend was wired back up to life.

It took him five more days to die of a racking
Pneumonia, never conscious but evidently
In horrid torment. The nurse had disappeared.
Did I hate her? Did I hate the friends
Who had involved me? Or hate myself
Who, like a slave lowering him into a pool
Of self-pity to make the poison work,
Had been forced to ask myself what to do?
And how in turn will I deal with the pain
Not of separation from but of attachment
To a body which has become a petulant
Tyrant? Whom will I ask to open the door
And discover me, to call out one last time
To the body lying there in a windowless room?

CAĞALOĞLU

From a cistern in the dome the daylight drips
        While the calls to prayer
    From the quarter's seven minarets—
Overlapping tape loops of Submission—slip
        Down through the arching crescent lunettes
        Cut into the air
As if the vault itself had loosened its grip.

I am on my back, listening to the tattoo
        Of clogs crisscrossing
    The sopping white marble floor inlaid
With veins of still darker matters to pursue.
        A skittish gleam accents, like eyeshade,
        A fountain's boss in
The corner alcove, where hot and cold make do

In a basin Tony Curtis and Franz Liszt
        Both stared into once.
    (Stardom is a predictable fate:
The point is forgotten but somehow still missed.)
        Gods, whenever they annunciate,
        Long for the romance
That ironclad heroes peering through the mist

Or mousy adolescent girls both provide.
        The same unlikely
    Places—a battlefield or grotto—
Are returned to, while again the hollow-eyed
        Ogle in flagrante devoto
        And obey, shyly,
The scrambled revelations so true-and-tried.

Congestive, crotch-scented vapor has congealed
Into beads that skid
Along suction-knots and shadow-ends
Abutting my slab. Eager for an ordeal
The illustrated brochure commends
As a bath to rid
The body of its filth both real and unreal,

I have bought their boast, "We make you feel reborn,"
For fifty euros.
Pinched and idly gestured toward a plinth
Two centuries of customers have careworn
To a shallow trough not quite my length,
I'm forced to burrow
Into a pose much more flagellant than faun.

The sodden towel is too heavy now to hold
Itself across me—
And there is the pasha's bay window,
The shriveled bulblet, the whole ill-shaped scaffold
Of surplus fact and innuendo,
From arthritic scree
To the congenital heart flutter's toehold.

The attendant walks up and down on my back,
Pacing the problem,
Then plucks, then mauls, then applies a foam
He scrubs in until it causes an attack
Of radiance, the world's palindrome
Suddenly solemn,
Suddenly seeming to surrender its knack

For never allowing us simply to want
                    What we already
              Have, or are, or perhaps could have been.
His hand-signal to get up seems like a taunt.
              I lie there, my fist under my chin,
                    Senses unsteady,
Something gradually, like a tiny font,

Coming into focus. I sit up and start
                    To notice small bits
              Of grit when I run my hand over
My chest. But wasn't this debris the chief part
              Of the package deal? The makeover
                    And its benefits?
In the fog I can't really see what trademark

Schmutz the Oriental Luxury Service
                    Has failed to wash off.
              So I put it in my mouth and taste
Two dank gobbets—salty, glairy, and grayish—
              I should have recognized as the waste
                    That was my old self,
A loofah having scraped it from each crevice

And bulge, from every salacious thought and deed.
                    Every good one too.
              It is the past, not just what is wrong,
It is the embarrassments we still breast-feed,
              That we absentmindedly so long
                    To shed. A new *you,*
Oneself an innate second person succeeds.

How do the saints feel when they fall to their knees,
                    God coming to light?
              Less ecstatic than ashamed, I fear,
Of bodies never worthy of being seized.
                   Encumbered by the weight of a tear,
                         In hopeless hindsight
They see all that the flesh can never appease,

All that the flesh is obliged to mortify.
                    Here I am, laid out,
               Looking up to where nothing appears,
Hardly wondering why nothing satisfies
                   And yet saddened that it's all so clear.
                        Tulip waterspouts
Trickle. Reservoirs deep underground reply.

from SCENES FROM
ANOTHER LIFE

1981

AUBADE

Snowbanks, so heaped by happenstance
A melting glance would misconstrue
Them as eiderdown, blanket the trails
Blazed, day in, night out, at dawn,

In dreams, whose patchwork accidents
Become the frosted dormer through
Brightening panes of which details
That make a world of sense are drawn.

A WINTER WITHOUT SNOW

Even the sky here in Connecticut has it,
That wry look of accomplished conspiracy,
The look of those who've gotten away

With a petty but regular white collar crime.
When I pick up my shirts at the laundry,
A black woman, putting down her *Daily News,*

Wonders why and how much longer our luck
Will hold. "Months now and no kiss of the witch."
The whole state overcast with such particulars.

For Emerson, a century ago and farther north,
Where the country has an ode's jagged edges,
It was "frolic architecture." Frozen blue-

Print of extravagance, shapes of a shared life
Left knee-deep in transcendental drifts:
The isolate forms of snow are its hardest fact.

Down here, the plain tercets of provision do,
Their picket snow-fence peeling, gritty,
Holding nothing back, nothing in, nothing at all.

Down here, we've come to prefer the raw material
Of everyday and this year have kept an eye
On it, shriveling but still recognizable—

A sight that disappoints even as it adds
A clearing second guess to winter. It's
As if, in the third year of a "relocation"

To a promising notch way out on the Sunbelt,
You've grown used to the prefab housing,
The quick turnover in neighbors, the constant

Smell of factory smoke—like Plato's cave,
You sometimes think—and the stumpy trees
That summer slighted and winter just ignores,

And all the snow that never falls is now
Back home and mixed up with other piercing
Memories of childhood days you were kept in

With a Negro schoolmate, of later storms
Through which you drove and drove for hours
Without ever seeing where you were going.

Or as if you've cheated on a cold sickly wife.
Not in some overheated turnpike motel room
With an old flame, herself the mother of two,

Who looks steamy in summer-weight slacks
And a parrot-green pullover. Not her.
Not anyone. But every day after lunch

You go off by yourself, deep in a brown study,
Not doing much of anything for an hour or two,
Just staring out the window, or at a patch

On the wall where a picture had hung for ages,
A woman with planets in her hair, the gravity
Of perfection in her features—oh! her hair

The lengthening shadow of the galaxy's sweep.
As a young man you used to stand outside
On warm nights and watch her through the trees.

You remember how she disappeared in winter,
Obscured by snow that fell blindly on the heart,
On the house, on a world of possibilities.

THE TEARS OF THE PILGRIMS

The gray figure whose back they are watching
Retreat down the stone passage where the river goes
Underground—an old man because he fails
To remember the recent, only the distant past—
Was telling the pilgrims of the grain
That takes for food the light that dies.
"I have stored sheaves of this death
Under the roof of my hunger,
And it has fed me."

.

There was no formal beginning,
No invocation, no lone patrol,
No offshore ceremonies of starting out,
Though each had a version of one,
Rich, contractual, obscure,
But missing the point
Even as it was being made
By insisting no one knew
Where it all would end, least of all
One like himself, a part of the story,
Black penitent, gradual saint.

.

Sunday. Tired of this leg of the journey,
I spent the morning in a field
Shot with broom and blooddrop poppies,
The clenched fists of thistle shaking.

Sat in a plot of clover flattened,
I guessed, by his animals. No company.
The sweet smell of grass on my sleeves.

Toward noon, two airplanes crossed
Over, high and dead ahead.
And once, somewhere near me,
A partridge made a noise
Like a blade being sharpened.

.

As if required by day-to-night necessities,
Or the custom of halting when the road
Led at last through the body's own fatigue,
We stayed a month in the Walled City,
Cloud banks toppling its outer defenses,
Toffee-brick roofs converting its allegory
Of crooked streets into a single allusion
That kept changing its mind as it was caught.

When the time came to leave, we paused
On the ancient splintered footbridge
For the only view of where we'd been.
Each saw something smaller than his sense
Of having been, having sheltered there.
A whole note held, galactic hive,
Emblematic welt of consequences unforeseen,
A paperweight village snowbound by a whim
Of the wrist, a case of mistaken identity,
An old engraving of Manhattan's reliquary
Of holy years on my own, when the griefs
Were never the same except in their origin,
Bold in trial, shy in isolation,

Heaped up with too many chances to take
Risks for, the humdrum deliberation
Of evenings and their standby reserves
Of permanence—belief, you called it,
In a future for the self beyond its task,
Its temporary ghosts, its squandered or hasty
Decisions to arrive, depart, to try again.

.

An invisible cloud lids
The moon's blind eye.

The owl's opens.

As if in response
To my unasked question,
He beats his wings,
Slowly at first,
Then faster and faster.

The moon starts up again.

That is more than God
Has ever said.

.

Stopping to admire the stream,
As if holding up its string of purls
To the light of his ability
To appreciate a pure style when he heard one,
He realized how clear the water had become
From wearing itself down on stones.

•

No plough, no wife, no child,
The four directions
Blow warm, blow cold;
The cricket sings to himself,
"Come, live in my house."

The rains start early,
The harvest comes late,
But I have a lucky guest;
We sit down tonight to lamb,
To garlic, salt, and wine.

The buried seed will sprout,
Will branch, will bear.
The southern hills stretch far
Away from where I search,
Stretch far away from here.

•

On the drive back across the border
After a cheap dinner in Spain,
The startling burst of bonfires—
Some in tenement courtyards,
But most in parking lots
Where anyone's car and orange crates
Burnt up and up into votive sparks—
Made us simultaneously afraid
And playful, as if (but by that time
Local friends in the backseat

Had explained tonight was St. John's Eve)
We too could have stopped to circle
Those shooting flames all night long.

．

When it was their turn to descend
The inverse spire of thresholds
And mainstays that closed in
On the cold breath at the bottom,
They waited, listening
To a short-winded cowbell first
Climb down its own hollow
Wooden overtones. Rung by rung
They followed, their feet soon used
To the drilled vermicular
Passage illuminated in a beam
Of lantern light the guide cast.

Filing down through tributaries
It seemed their hearts had divided
Into, summoned to ten springs
Of pain and joy at the summit
Of a cry carried to the very center
Of a gathering universal emptiness,
They grew absorbed by the dark face
That led them on. Missing front tooth,
Red shirt rolled up on writhing tattoos,
Young enough to mask his self-possession,
And old enough to conjure up the myth
Of a boy, a boatman, a bereavement.

Hand over hand, he pulled the launch
Along the river by grips hammered into
The runneling cave at intervals
Between some new contrivance
Of time collapsed in stone—drapery,
Hogshead, needle pavilion, cascade
Accumulated since the muse first sang
In the steadfast informing trill of water
The boy, in his language, called
"Falling angels," each dropped down
Into this vast freezing echo
Of themselves as they left the air.

•

There was no finding their way
Through the pass that morning or next.
(Years ago this was when it happened.)
The flat valley floor, its scrub brush
And laurel, its dusty copperplated prairie,
Too abruptly gave way—and within sight
Of the other side—to sheer crags
Glowering as they disappeared behind
Overlapping jadeite scrolls of fog
On which was written nothing but
The tingling silence they stood in,
Slept in, woke in with what misgivings,
What intermittent attempts at self-effacement
They couldn't have understood until now.

•

They can all but see the dimpled smiles
Break up the clear reflecting pool

From the depths of which others reach
Their infant fingers towards them.

Or toward a homelike roof overhead,
The nightsky lit by fate's maternal fires.

•

The night before they arrived
They took separate rooms
The better to ponder each
His own solitude long after
It was probable, they'd been told,
Either would be alone again.
No more the rigors of endless
Possibility remote from love
Yet closer to an exacting idea
Of some imagined mark—
The weeping flight of cranes,
Or the plash of an oar
Opening petal by petal,
A deliquescent lily floating
On the swell of a response.

Instead, the pair's ardent plight,
Twinned complexity of pattern
And overcharged resource
Pledged to far-reaching years,
With little opportunity to ask
For more than would find itself
In reach. A constant expectation,
Common table, late hours at rest.

One closed his eyes, thought
Of his dead friends, of rotting
Masterpieces, their hopes,
The whispering shrine of sudden
Death in which they meditated
On its available mode of infinity.
There was no need to go further
With the arbitrary rules.
He opened his eyes, thought

Write the book
                  in your hearts.
Lose no time.

And the other, bewildered by himself,
Watched out the window,
Cracked through a diamond diagonal
Whose faults kept doubling the stars.

from STARS PRINCIPAL

1986

AT A READING

Anthony Hecht's

And what if now I told you this, let's say,
By telephone. Would you imagine me
Talking to myself in an empty room,
Watching myself in the window talking,
My lips moving silently, birdlike,
On the glass, or because superimposed
On it, among the branches of the tree
Inside my head? As if what I had to say
To you were in these miniatures of the day,
When it is last night's shadow shadows
Have made bright.
                    Between us at the reading—
You up by that child's coffin of a podium,
The new poem, your "Transparent Man," to try,
And my seat halfway back in the dimmed house—
That couple conspicuous in the front row
You must have thought the worst audience:
He talked all the while you read, she hung
On *his* every word, not one of yours.
The others, rapt fan or narcolept,
Paid their own kind of attention, but not
Those two, calm in disregard, themselves
A commentary running from the point.
Into putdown? you must have wondered,
Your poem turned into an example, the example
Held up, if not to scorn, to a glaring
Spot of misunderstanding, some parody
Of the original idea, its afterlife
Of passageways and the mirrory reaches
Of beatitude where the dead select

Their patience and love discloses itself
Once and for all.
                    But you kept going.
I saw you never once look down at them,
As if by speaking *through* her you might
Save the girl for yourself and lead her back
To *your* poem, *your* words to lose herself in,
Who sat there as if at a bedside, watching,
In her shift of loud, clenched roses, her hands
Balled under her chin, the heart in her throat
All given in her gaze to the friend
Beside her. How clearly she stood out
Against everything going on in front of us.

It was then I realized that she was deaf
And the bearded boy, a line behind you,
Translating the poem for her into silence,
Helping it out of its disguise of words,
A story spilled expressionless from the lip
Of his mimed exaggerations, like last words
Unuttered but mouthed in the mind and formed
By what, through the closed eyelid's archway,
Has been newly seen, those words she saw
And seeing heard—or not heard but let sink in,
Into a darkness past anyone's telling,
There between us.
                    What she next said,
The bald childless woman in your fable,
She said, head turned, out the window
Of her hospital room to trees across the way,
The leaflorn beech and the sycamores
That stood like enlargements of the vascular
System of the brain, minds meditating on
The hill, the weather, the storm of leukemia

In the woman's bloodstream, the whole lot
Of it "a riddle beyond the eye's solution,"
These systems, anarchies, ends not our own.

The girl had turned her back to you by then,
Her eyes intent on the thickness of particulars,
The wintery emphasis of that woman's dying,
Like facing a glass-bright, amplified stage,
Too painful not to follow back to a source
In the self. And like the girl, I found myself
Looking at the boy, your voice suddenly
Thrown into him, as he echoed the woman's
Final rendering, a voice that drove upward
Onto the lampblack twigs just beyond her view
To look back on her body there, on its page
Of monologue. The words, as they came—
Came from you, from the woman, from the voice
In the trees—were his then, the poem come
From someone else's lips, as it can.

THE CUP

The figures on this morning's second cup
Slowly wake to a touch whose method
Varies. My finger's circling outside the fire-
Charged sunrise saucer and the cloud
Chip on its rim, while the sugary anthem
Of dregs inside, struck up to call a halt

To dreaming, turns strangely bitter. Halting,
Blind, it's they who finger the lip of the cup.
Hoplite or sharecropper, can I speak for them?
A grown-up love asks a relentless method.
They swarm like ghosts to the bloody cloud
Of thought: what of *my* life, where's *my* fire?

One of them bends now to spit in the fire.
The only hesitation is of flame, its halt
Or stutter, as when the heart bolts out of a cloud
Long enough to light what's fallen to the cup's
Dark side to show, illustration's methodical
Storm of types. Two chances. Which of them

Is mine? The horse and rider's winded anthem?
Or the thumbprint ash, arms akimbo, blackfired
Against the light? Oh, love's our method
To let blood put on the skyspan halter,
That bit of thinking, then ride, then cup
The dawn in a cold hand. The cloud

Parts again. Moon mouth half shut on cloud.
Star crumbs. A woman rising to leave them
To themselves. She's overturned their cup
Of responsibilities, spilling it into the fire's

Airglow. And when she asked whose fault
It was, I had to choose between old methods

Of excess. You'll hear I chose that myth odd
To some, even to her, and know how it would cloud
Any fear of hers to make time pass or halt
On that one moment. The myth holds one of them—
I mean now one of us—up to the fire
Already gone out from the body, as into a cup,

Its thirsts poured into another cup, a method
To balance the fire's given set of words, a cloud
That drifts over them before it halts at *sorrow*.

ANTHEM

All things began in separation: the day's
Young god, puffed, fireshod, first dispatched
On a mirrored globe: the negress, locked up
In a star chamber, her lamp at the lone window:
Dry land parted from sea, its bulbous fruit
Spilt from river urns, the spring's leaking
Pitcher drawn up from the airy stream: wave's
Spume breaks on a caudal fin, shells soften
To paws: then the clouds too will take shape
As stag and hen, infant owl who repeats—*who?*

Made of something missing, the couple comes:
His city in flames, a stitch in his side
From having run this far away from home,
He dreams his heart's a book, open to her
Taper's hovering wing: call him again:
He had not meant so much he could not see
The worst that love can do: to wake and leave
Loving, indifferent to practice this one way:
But who will believe me if I say he fell
Into some deeper sleep: in the end was a word.

THE PALACE DWARF

The Ladder of Paradise would lead, this time,
    To the Apartment of the Dwarfs, the steps
        So short the rise was gradual as an afterlife.
    The French looked at pictures in their guidebooks
        As it was described. The Germans whispered
Loudly to each other. I watched the dwarf

Climb the stairs. I had spotted him the day before,
    Flat on a wall by the Mincio, reading *Emma*.
        That was put aside, some scenes too clogged
    With allusion, like the river with its frisbees,
        Detergent jugs, weeds in cellophane barrettes.
But here he was again. No gainsaying the insistent,

Good and evil alike. Which did he seem, in sunglasses,
    A studded motorcycle jacket, smudge of sideburns,
        Tattooed crown of thorns? His baby-head
    Bulged with its one secret, how to turn anyone's
        Gold back into straw, this whole palace—
Ticket-booth, fresco, tourist group, the long galleries

Overthrown with history—into a dropcloth, a slatting
    Canvas yanked aside from plaster-frame ambition,
        The heart made small with scorn of littleness.
    Did he feel at home here, where only he could
        Fit? But who ever does? Head bowed now
In self-defense, I followed him up the tilting

Scale, from the chapel, its breadbox altar and gnarled
    Crucified savior, in death near lifesized for him,
        Back to the bedrooms and the favorite's gilded
    Manger. Not a word, not a wink. He took it all in,

Or all but what was missing, any window view
That gave out on "the former owner's" contradictions,

A garden's logic of originality, the box-hedged
    Bets, the raging winged cypresses, the royal
        Children playing with their head-on-a-stick,
    The jester's marotte, over whose cap they'd look
        Back, up at the Apartment, that skewed cortex
Through which I wormed behind him. How close

It had suddenly become, when as if into the daylight
    That jabs a shut eye from between the curtains
        Of his dream, we were led into the next room,
    Where guardian archers had once been posted,
        Their crossbows ready for the unseen nod,
Their forty horses stabled in paint above.

Each niche turned a knotted tail impatiently.
    Instinct looks up. But where one expected
        Allegory, the simple bearings that tell us
    Where and how tall we ought to stand—some titan
        Routing the pygmy appetites, some child
Humbling kings to their senses—the ceiling's frame

Of reference was empty—the missing window at last?—
    Clouds bearing nothing. And nothing was what
        We were certain of. We looked around
    For the dwarf, the moral of these events.
        He was waddling out of a far door, as if
He knew where next we all would want to be.

A COLD IN VENICE

Montaigne—for him the body of knowledge
Was his own, to be suffered or studied
Like a local custom—had one too, I read
In bed, his diary more alert and all-gathering
The more I lose touch with it, or everything.
Even the gardenia on the neighbor's sill
That for three nights running a nightingale
Has tended with streamsprung song—
The senses competing with a giddy vulgarity—
Draws a blank. The San Vio vesper bells
Close in, fade, close in, then fade
To the congestion of voices from the street.

Why "clear as a bell"? Even as the time-release
Capsule I'm waiting on is stuffed with pellets
The bell must first be choked with the changes
To be rung, all there at once, little explosions
Of feeling, the passages out of this world.

These pills clear a space, as if for assignment
Undercover. Last week's liver seared in oil
And sage, the mulberry gelato on the Zattere . . .
Neither smell nor taste make it back.
And what of the taste for time itself,
Its ravelled daybook and stiff nightcap,
What it clears from each revisited city,
Depths the same, no inch of surface unchanged?
I can see to that. The gouged pearl pattern
Of light on the canals, the grimy medallioned
Cavities of the facings, or goldleaf phlegm
Around a saint's head. It's always something
About the body. For Montaigne the cure

Was "Venetian turpentine"—grappa, no doubt—
Done up in a wafer on a silver spoon.
The next morning he noticed the smell
Of March violets in his urine.

                              How dependent
One becomes on remedies, their effects familiar
As a flower's perfumed throat, or a bird's
Thrilled questioning, like the trace
Of a fingertip along that throat, or now
Between the lines of a book by someone well
I'd taken up to read myself asleep with.

THE LESSON IN PREPOSITIONS

de

The night watchman, Mr. Day,
having let us in, the elevator's
pneumatic breath is held,
counting now again to ten.
It's we who wonder what's up.
Arriving there follows after
a loss—is it of that push-
button Panic, or Power's pulley?—
over any grounds for leaving.
The rule is, if you try to hurt
by silence, you'll find the words
to accuse yourself of speech.
Time to talk back. Say *here, out.*
The fingertipped light's gone out.

ex

Because the door automatically slid
closed against a pointless kiss—
an ashen sulphur-bulb still smoking—
and by reason of a walk refused
out of a mood since despaired of
for effects . . . no, wait for me!
If you'll apologize, I'll go.

sine

The way the dead live in dreams
as ageless ego's poor relation,
the milksop or wattled Muscovy duck,
every feature, under a merciful eye,
concentrated on "Did you *ever* love me?"
—so there you are, without an answer.

sub

My friend the screenwriter,
the moth in Armani fatigues
under cover of flickering credits,
is in from the coast and down
on his luck. "You've no idea
what it's like to loll
in the hold. The whisperjet
full of studio spies could talk
of nothing else." At the foot of having
been left to myself, I could
only think of our old days out back,
Vantages lit, the stock company
of headmasters left to the dishes.
We were playing the Landscape Game.
House. Key. Body of water. Beast.
A bowl stood in for art. Yours
had legs that ran all the way home.
It was a backdoor in summer,
your mother calling through
the half-patched screen. The fireflies
in your jar brightened when you shook.

ad

The new stars are coming out.
To ward off another influence
is one priority, but only one.
The other is to catch their light
as a design on us, then call it
hardship up among the heroes.
I go back to what falls
out as advance. Call their bluff
a cloud that blurs the dark
retreating densities. Or call it
hardship, then call to it again
and hear answer: *come up here*
and see for yourself. Even then
I went ahead and answered back.
Who has the last word wins
his forced smile, but only one.

cum

With what? The too familiar
self that ducks behind depressions,
a cigarette and shot on the stoop?
The estranged hubbub of dressing?
How often can one ask, how
do I look? I look alone,
perched in this mare's nest
of cross-hatched fume and twig.
The newel-post could be a trunk
(packed with, oh, rings of age)
to climb back down on.
This once there's a footstep,
an echo, a step, then a step.

pro

As good as guilt in front
of his floor-length plea
for the short view of sincerity,
even the blackest has side.
When he's right, I'm left
donned in flawless arraignment.

post

What's over takes the accusative,
shears to the podded scape, shovel
down on the woodchuck's skull,
the humbling touch, or misfingered
bagatelle that bears down not on
but as the moment. The point's
to add dependence whether or not
you have the means to support it,
a pedal weight that sticks,
like blood, like brooding,
to make a fool of motive,
love's long held embarrassment.

BEES

First to bloom at last
    this late spring
the crabapple's a wain
    of white the ox
sun is hauling homeward.

Humbles brawl on top,
    goaded by syrups,
the rut of work so far
    from the wing-lit
hive of their making.

A bent toward folly argues
    for intelligence.
They'll break with the past
    as with an enemy.
The flowers cry to them!

•

Left behind, in clover's
    common sense,
a solitary honeybee
    plies her trade.
Circumspect, all twelve

thousand eyes are trained
    on her needlework:
genetic cross-stitch
    and pollen purl.
Her pattern is the field's.

HUMMINGBIRD

There is no hum, of course, nor is the bird
That shiver of stained glass iridescence
Through which the garden appears—itself
In flight not from but toward an intensity
Of outline, color, scent, each flower
An imperium—as in a paragraph of Proust.

Mine is a shade of that branch it rests on
Between rounds: bark-wing, lichen-breast,
The butternut's furthest, hollow twig.
How to make from sow thistle to purslane?
So, into this airy vault of jewelweed,
Slipped past the drowsing bee watch,

Deep into the half-inch, bloodgold
Petal curve, tongue of the still untold.
Deaf to tones so low, the bees never mind
The dull grinding, these rusted gears
Pushed to the limit of extracting
From so many its little myth of rarity.

OVID'S FAREWELL

What was my fault? A book, and something I saw.
    The one he never read, the other
        He was author of.
    Not his daughter—her adulteries
    Were with boys from other men's beds, mine
Merely with women from other men's poems—

But his empire. He had long since made his Peace
    And thereby the fear that would keep it,
        The commerce of praise
    And the short sword, a vomit that cleanses
    The palate. The same horses that tear
The flesh at night by day drive over the tribes.

The quarry falls into his toils. We all have
    Our methods of conquest. Even me.
        Mine was the dove-drawn
    Chariot named Illusion, cockeyed
    Laurel crown, and whispers on the way.
I could have chosen another theme—the sons

Who kill their fathers, the brothers who salt each
    Other's cities, or the empire's spawn,
        Glistered avenues
    To sacrifice, bloody baths and nets.
    But mine was love-in-idleness scratched
On an apple. In that sweet anatomy

Of desire he smells a treason. Woodland
      Shrines and pillow-books, the subversive
            Mirror, its fragrant
      Incestuous tear beneath the bark—
      These conspire against the down-turned
Thumb, policy for sale with chalk on its feet

And locks around its heels. When gods make themselves
      Into men, they become less than men,
            A human desire.
      When men would be gods, they pass new laws
      And strengthen the Family. Like gods,
Then, they breed contempt and their own betrayal.

Though whatever work I tried turned under me
      Into verse, the spells and bullroarers
            Of family life
      Resisted all but a low satire,
      The cold late supper of everyday.
I had chosen and loved a life in the shade,

A cough, certain oils, her blue lips from under.
      It was from such shadows that I saw
            His daughter come to
      Kick against his rule. I ignored her,
      Of course, but one of her slaves had seen
Me, and seen a way to pay for his freedom.

Slaves, our living shades, are like readers, always
      Eager for a new master. Lovers
            Look for somewhere else
      To live, and when they find it, they ask
      The poet for passage. Now it is
My turn to pay for love. First my poems made me

Friends, now fame has made my enemies. Tomis?
    In Greek the word means "amputation"
        And so he would have
    My tongue cut out. The title is his,
    Not mine, called the Master of Changes.
The life to come will be all the past, the world

Before Rome, rough skins and grunts and frenzied wasps
    In their rain-ruined tents. I hear they
        Have only one god
    To worship. How can one god fill up
    The sky? Or answer for this wrangle
In the heart? Perhaps the sky there in Tomis—

Where the Kid is drowned under waves, and the Bear
    Kept chained to his pole—is small enough.
        I am to be changed
    Into a *character*—a woman
    Whose lover is at wine and gaming
With knuckle-bones. She smears her eyes with charcoal

So he will not see her—if he should look up—
    Looking away. Or, if not that girl,
        Then what is the same,
    A ghost, skirling inside an urn called
    Tomis. Flattery! That is the work
Of a woman and a ghost. Let us play them

Tonight, before I am both, and you neither.
    My friends tell me, Fabia, I am
        Married to story,
    And so to change. But men do not change,
    They grow old, and grow afraid. I have
Left wives before, but not one I loved. There, there,

. . . The very poem of Troy is enacted!
    The fires wept on, the hearth gods smashed,
        The old queen's ashes
    Passed from hand to hair. They are afraid
    For themselves, my friends, and come to offer
Advice like gentlemen. I may as well count

On the critics. Not that I mind to beg them
    For it. Their pity is a fool's gold
        And dealt in Caesar-
    Struck coin. One will pay my ferry-ride.
    But what shall I take from this last night?
A book? A strong leather cloak? A pen to blind

Myself with petitions? We all live someone
    Else's story, so we may know how
        It turns out. I have
    Taken something before, then . . . But what?
    My brother's life. Yes. No one knows that,
Nor ever thought it then, thirty years ago.

One day, in an island of wheatspikes,
    We were playing our war, his mattock
        Up in the noonlight's
    Angry hour, my barrel-siding
    Like an elephant on the mountain.
Having leaped into some last ditch of defense,

His angular stillness was itself both call
    And surrender. Not meant to win,
        I wondered, then saw
    The snake, black standard of an army
    Marching off under the world. I watched
Its tongue question the distance to the boy.

When it stopped, the tale came to my lips. "Brother,
 Show respect to the god, a sea-borne
  God, come to favor—"
 My own panic made up its mission—
 "The purple shells on his cave's ceiling
Were tongues that told of the Sun's only daughter

Who kept his light from the dead, their souls the chaff
 Winnowed from life. If a snake could slip
  Into the mill's pin. . . ."
 Calmed, I continued, and backed away.
 He turned to me, as one who believes
Will turn the page, and as he turned, the snake struck.

The stone in my throat was that one said
 To turn black in the hand of a liar.
  Dog's milk was rubbed on
 His gums, a wolf's liver in thin wine
 Was forced, and cow dung through a fresh reed.
Superstitions save what's no longer wanted.

He died. He died as silent as I've remained.
 The next day I dreamed the god came back,
  Had truly returned
 And come to the chamber of the dead.
 My brother, pale as a grain fallen
On a cloth, recognized him and stood, head bowed,

Intent on his part. Then the god took him up
 To Hercules whose quiver behind
  Is a crown of stars.
 But the great Serpent coiled in night,
  As the boy approached, wound itself round
The hero's outstretched arm who was to hold

Him fast by his side, a friend to his labors.
So the boy in error was taken
Further up, farther
Away, too far to be seen by men.
But I have, there between the bowstring
And the shaft, whenever I look up for a line.

Exile—a boy into death, the bit of life
Stranded in a song, or its singer—
Is the end of our
Belief. It comes to pass, the last change
As the first, from a stream of star-shot
Wonderment that falls down to our home on earth.

from THE REST OF THE WAY

1990

MEDEA IN TOKYO

Already in place, her tears are chainlink gold,
Her grief a silken streamer of "blood" that friends
Draw slowly from her mouth while she is told
A rival has worked her magic. Who's the witch?
The unseen girl will have her hour, then ends
Up on fire. And the star's in fact an old
Man, with clay breasts and trailing robe
Forty pounds of mirror flints enrich,
Who never says a word I comprehend.

What happens when the language is a mask,
And the words we use to hush this up have failed?
The chorus—beekeepers with samisens—ask
That question (I think) over and over again.
Is tragedy finally wrenched from fairy tale
When we ought to understand but can't pretend?

She doesn't hear a thing. Her dragon cart—
The bucket of a sleek hydraulic lift—
Sways above us all. By now the part
Has worn out her revenge. We're made to feel
Even she is beyond the spell of speech, the gift
Of fate she gave the others. But a moral starts
To echo. The children's screams. And to each wheel
A body's tied with ribbons, pale and stiff.
The words had made no sense, but the sword was real.

THE RENTED HOUSE

The faintly digital click of the overhead fan
    stroking what was left of the dark
      had finally given way to a rooster alarm.
        Not that we needed one.

We'd been kept awake all night by cats, cats
    in the crawlspace, in the yard,
      up and down the back lane, until it seemed
        they were in your head,

their guttural chittering, then a courting sound—
    more like tires spinning on ice—
      a sort of erotic simmer that would mount
        to a wail in heat, a wailing,

one pair, and soon after another, the same,
    sex shrieking all around and under us,
      who hadn't touched, or barely spoken, for days.
        When I leaned over you

to bang on the window, your back was hot on my chest.
    I banged louder, longer, less to scare
      the cats away than to feel your heat, the flesh
        and an inch above the flesh,

while listening to theirs, though theirs hurt less
    because the pain thrilled, you could hear it,
      the now worried tom helplessly caught in her
        until she'd had enough.

And then they set to fighting. Again and again
        I'd be getting out of bed to stamp or shout
    into the dark, and they would stop for a minute
            before turning on each other

with a threatening sigh-long cough. No point, no use
        trying to silence it. And the losers,
    self-pitying, moved off further under the house,
            making a curious new sound,

a wounded coo and some hen-gabble (Christ!
        I should have known that rooster was a cat).
    By morning we were all exhausted, trying to start
            something or stop it,

giving in to another day, angry—but angry at what?
        There on the porch, when I opened the screen door,
    a black, three-legged, pregnant cat was sitting,
            our brooding household god,

last night's own story staring back at me in the slatted
        early palmlight, all the accidents of envy and will
    thrown together in one mangled, swollen creature,
            mewling, limping, her stump

dangling down beneath her belly. When I took one,
        then two hesitant steps toward her, she arched
    and hobbled away. Sometimes a life comes to its senses,
            or suddenly just speeds up,

as when we first met, whole months it seemed collapsed
        to a night, an emptiness years-deep filled
    and spilling over by dawn into—but first things first.
            Some milk. A shallow bowl.

By the time I'd returned with it, the cat had vanished.
But there beside the door, earlier overlooked,
you'd already set a milkbowl down for her yourself,
someone else's earthenware,

the glazed, coarse-grained gesture neither of us
can make for each other. Poor, stupid cat,
where are you? All day the bowls have sat there,
side by side, untouched.

THE SHIELD OF HERAKLES

The ocean circles its outer rim,
With dented silver swan-shaped studs
To hold taut the backing, deerskin
Lashed to a frame of olive wood.

Next, as if on shore, a round
Of horsemen, loosening their reins,
Gaining on a prize forever unwon.
The face of each is worked in pain.

(Who once coughed up the Milky Way
And later, maddened, killed his sons
Has guiltily now to undertake
Labors to please a weaker man.)

And then a city with seven gates
Of gold where men are bringing home
A bride in her high-wheeled chariot.
Shrill bridal pipes and their echo

Mingle with the swollen torches,
Women, one foot lifted to the lyre,
And a pack of young men watching
Or laughing in the dance, tired,

Others mounted, galloping past
A field the ploughman's just turned up.
Sharpened hooks have reaped the last
Bending stalks that children prop

In sheaves. Beside them now a row
Of vines, with ivory tendrils curled
On grapes soon trod upon to draw
Their sweetness for the frightened girl.

(My journal of dreams this month: "One
By one the twelve new monsters yield."
The doctor says the threat's begun
To counterattack. Is strength a shield?)

Deeper within stand ranks of men
In warring harness, to hold or sack
The town, while corpses, enemy by friend,
Lie near widows tearing their cheeks—

They could have been alive. The Fates,
Shrouded in black enamel, loom
Behind, clawing a soldier to taste
The blood that drips from an open wound.

And closer still four faces stare—
Panic, Slaughter, Chaos, Dread—
Each knotted to the next one's hair
By serpents, like the Gorgon's head.

And here are souls now swept beneath
The world, all made of palest glass,
Their skin and bones long since bequeathed
To earth, where the wandering stars pass.

(The archers squint at a gleaming phalanx,
As if from nowhere moved into place.
Machine-made Armageddons—tanks
Or missile shields in outer space—

Threaten always to turn against
The false-hearted power they excite.
What draws attack is self-defense,
A target for the arrow's flight.)

And at its very center, a wonder
Held up to see, the figure of Fear
Was hammered fast by fire and thunder.
But only half her face appears.

The other half is turned away,
A quivering lip, one widened eye,
Turned back as if to warn in vain
The armored giant, come to rely

On what protects to terrify,
That while at night his dreams explain
The city and field, the dance, the bride,
A crow is picking at one of the slain.

FOG TROPES

A sheet of water turned over.
Sedge script. River erasure.
The smoke out of the factory
Stacks drifts to the title page—
Words too big to read, too quickly
Gone to say what they are.
The water turbine is stalled
And sighs. There go last night's
Now forgotten dreams, airborne,
Homebound, on their way to work.

.

Again this morning: five-storey elm spoons
Stirring the wheylight, fur on the knobby
Melon rind left in the sink, the china egg
Under the laying hen, the quilt's missing
Patch, and now the full moon's steamed-up
Shaving mirror leaning against the blue.

.

When my daughter died, from the bottom
Of every pleasure something bitter
Rose up, a sour taste of nausea,
The certain sense of having failed
Not to save her but in the end to know
I could not keep her from passing
As through the last, faintest intake
Of breath to somewhere unsure of itself,
The dim landscape that grief supposes.
I remember how, in the hospital,

Without a word she put her glasses on
And stared ahead, just before she died.

I take mine off these days, to see
More of my solitude, its incidental
Humiliations. Nothing satisfies
Its demand that she appear in order
To leave my life over and over again.
If, from my car, I should glimpse her
In a doorway, bright against the dark
Inside, and stop and squint at the glare—
It's a rag on a barbed-wire fence.
Or I spot her in a sidewalk crowd
But almost at once she disappears
The way one day slips behind the next.
I've come to think of her now, in fact,
Or of her ghost I guess you'd have to say,
As the tear that rides and overrides
My eye, so that the edges of things go
Soft, a girl is there and not there.

.

Even in the dark
The long shadow of the stars
Drifts beneath the pines.

.

Snagged on a stalk: fresh tufts of rabbit down,
Thistle silk, a thumbnail's lot of spittle spawn.

.

Fidgeting among the goateed professors
And parlor radicals at the *Pension Russe,*
The girls whispered to themselves
About the tubercular young Reinhard,
Alone at a corner table, smoking,
Who had introduced them to immortality
By burning a cigarette paper
And as the ash plummeted upward
Exclaiming *"Die Seele fliegt!"*

.

It's the first breath of the dead
That rises from the firing squad
While the anarchist who squealed
Gets drunk and argues with God.

It's Shelley's lung in the lake
And his hand in the ashes on shore.
It's the finespun shirt he ordered
And the winding sheet he wore.

.

When the two famous novelists discovered
Each the other in the same dress—
A shot-silk "creation" of orris-dust
Laid on blanched silver, like the irony
That is the conscience of style, obscuring
To clarify, bickering to be forgiven—
One retired with her pale young admirers,
Disdain for whom creamed up in her tea,
To a folly by the buckled apple tree.
She sat and pretended to listen to herself

Being praised, picking at grizzled lichen
On the bench, like drops of blistered enamel.
The other tugged at her pearls and stayed
Near the smiles, her dress insinuated
Among the lead crystal teardrops
On the fixture above her, each one
The size, and now the color, of a blossom
On an apple bough outside, and herself
Inside, tiny and helplessly upsidedown.

                    •

The first month of the first marriage.
The second year of the second marriage.
The third betrayal of the third marriage.
And love. Love. Always love.

                    •

a deep winter yawn
                            the wind caught napping
static on the news
                            charred ozone glaze
dead-petal weather
                            the air's loose skin
the albino's birthmark
                            the vinegar mother
a bubble in the artery
                            the pebble in Demosthenes' mouth
love asleep at the wheel
                            childhood stunned and dumped
the philosopher's divorce
                            the psychopomp's coin
self-pity's last tissue

                    the blister on the burn
        the emptiness added daily
                    the abstract's arsenal
        quarry of doubts
                    earthrise from the dark side
        the holy sleeve
                    the beatific blindness
        white root of heaven
                    the hedge around happiness

        •

The sound of it? A silence
Understood as all the noise
Ignored or stifled, nods
Exchanged on the trading floor,
Or sex in the next room,
His hand over her mouth,
Her belt, the overcast leather,
Clenched between his teeth.
Where the needle stuck,
Its hiss and hard swallow
Halfway into the heart
Of the nocturne, two notes
Fell further apart, the space
Between them a darkness
Clotting, the moon
Having passed behind
A black key, then risen
Higher across the record's
Rutted, familiar road.

        •

Suddenly, lengths of storm gauze
Drawn across the clearing.
We must not want too much
To know. Uncertainty
Condenses on the windshield,
Then runs down the cheek,
A single waxen tear.
When last night's grief
Is pulled back from,
Who will be the brighter?
Hush. Be careful. Turn
Those headlights down, low
As a curtained candle flame
Shivering in the dark dispelled.

.

First, the diagnosis: those night sweats
And thrush, the breathing that misplaces air,
The clouds gathering on a horizon of lung . . .
Translated as *pneumocystis,* the word from a dead
Language meant to sound like a swab
On a wound open but everywhere unseen.
Then, the options. There were options,
Left like food trays outside your door.
Protocols, support groups, diets,
A promising treatment.
                              But three months later
You began to forget the doctor's appointments,
And the next week no longer cared that you forgot.
The friends who failed to visit, even their letters
Grew hard to parse. It was not as if their "real"
Feelings lay between the lines, but that the lines
Themselves would break apart: *the fight so long*

All your work   the circumstances   remember when.
But remember was precisely what you couldn't do,
And to pay attention more than you could afford.
The books you'd read now looked back at you
With blank pages memories might fill in
With makeshift, events haphazardly recalled—
Snow swarming on the canal that Christmas
In Venice with Claudio who cried to see it,
Or globes of watery sunlight in your Chelsea flat,
White lilacs at their lips last May, no one there
For a change but just you two.
                                    And here you are
Still, propped up in the half-light, my shadow,
My likeness, your hand wandering to the arm
Of the chair, as if your fingers might trace
The chalkdust of whole years erased.
Is this, then, what it means to lose your life?
But the question is forgotten before it can be
Answered. I take your hand, and give it back
To you, and watch you then look up, giving in,
Unknowing all, whose pain has just begun.

HEADS

As if layered in a wedge of honey cake,
    The aromas of split persimmon,
        Mint, cat spray, and cardamom
    All mingle with the bitter coffee
        On this morning's scuffed brass tray
Brought into the shop by a cripple with wings.

The match for two Marlboros also now strikes
    The end to one loud bit of holy
        ("Faith" in Arabic is *din*)
    Bargaining at the end of the street.
        Peels of old light lie scattered
Outside. Dogs barking. Market day in the souk.

Muhammad deals in goat heads. His rival's shop
    Is beef, swags of lung and counters heaped
        With livers like paving stones,
    A child-high pile of squat, outsize shins
        And marbleized, harelipped hearts—
Food the rich man eats to settle his conscience.

And there are flies next door, and a hose to wash
    Dung out of the cow guts . . . which reminds
        Muhammad of his brother
    Who left to become headwaiter at
        Rasputin's Piano-Bar.
Both his grandfathers, his father too, had worked

In this tiled hollow lit by one bare bulb.
        Stuck in the mirror are their postcards
            Of the Kaaba, the silk-veiled,
        Quartz-veined sky-stone, Islam's one closed eye.
            Muhammad hasn't made his
Required pilgrimage. He went west instead,

The hajj to California, but came up six
        Credits shy at Fresno State. (Shy too
            Of the girlfriend who'd wanted
        To marry "for good," not a green card.)
            So he's back in the shop now,
Next to a copper tub of boiling water.

He takes another head by the ear and dips
        It—*eight, nine, ten*—into the kettle,
            Then quickly starts to shave it
        With a bone-handled wartime Gillette.
            The black matted shag falls in
Patches to the floor and floats toward the clogged drain.

One after another, the heads are stacked up
        Behind, like odd-lot, disassembled
            Plastic replicas of goats.
        Though their lips are hardened now, the teeth
            Of some can be seen—perfect!
But Muhammad hacks the jaws off anyway,

And the skulls with their nubbly horns and ears.
        What's left is meant for his faithful poor,
            For their daily meager stew.
        He lines up six on a shelf out front.
            (As if all turned inside out,
The heads, no longer heads exactly, strangely

Bring to mind relief maps of the "occupied
　　　Territories." Born on the wrong side
　　　　　Of a new border, he's made
　　　To carry his alien's ID,
　　　　　Its sullen headshot labeled
In the two warring tongues.) Goat heads feel them all,

The refugee, the single man, and his dog—
　　　Their delicacy. Cartilage knobs.
　　　　　Fat sacs. The small cache of flesh.
　　　The eyeballs staring out at nothing
　　　　　In all directions. The tongue
Lolling up, as if with something more to say.

Jerusalem, November 1987

AN ESSAY ON FRIENDSHIP

Friendship is love without wings.
—FRENCH PROVERB

I.

Cloud swells. Ocean chop. Exhaustion's
Black-and-white. The drone at last picked up
By floodlights a mile above Le Bourget.

Bravado touches down. And surging past
Police toward their hero's spitfire engine,
His cockpit now become the moment's mirror,

The crowd from inside dissolves to flashbulbs.
Goggles, then gloves, impatiently pulled off,
He climbs down out of his boy's-own myth.

His sudden shyness protests the plane deserves
The credit. But his eyes are searching for a reason.
Then, to anyone who'd listen: "She's not here?

But . . . but I flew the Atlantic because of her."
At which broadcast remark, she walks across
Her dressing room to turn the radio off.

Remember how it always begins? The film,
That is. *The Rules of the Game,* Renoir's tragi-
Comedy of manners even then

Outdated, one suspects, that night before
The world woke up at war and all-for-love
Heroes posed a sudden risk, no longer

A curiosity like the silly marquis's
Mechanical toys, time's fools, his stuffed
Warbler or the wind-up blackamoor.

Besides, she prefers Octave who shared those years,
From twelve until last week, before and after
The men who let her make the mistakes she would

The morning after endlessly analyze—
This puzzle of a heart in flight from limits—
With her pudgy, devoted, witty, earthbound friend.

II.

—A friend who, after all, was her director,
Who'd written her lines and figured out the angles,
Soulful *auteur* and comic relief in one,

His roles confused as he stepped center-stage
(Albeit costumed as a performing bear)
From behind the camera—or rather, out

Of character. Renoir later told her
The question "how to belong, how to meet"
Was the film's only moral preoccupation,

A problem the hero, the Jew, and the woman share
With the rest of us whose impulsive sympathies
For the admirable success or loveable failure

Keep from realizing the one terrible thing
Is that everyone has his own good reasons.
The husband wants the logic of the harem—

I.e., no one is thrown out, no one hurt—,
His electric organ with its gaudy trim and come-on,
Stenciled nudes. His wife, who's had too much

To drink, stumbles into the château's library
And searches for a lover on the shelf just out
Of reach, the one she learned by heart at school.

The lover, meanwhile (our aviator in tails)
Because love is the rule that breaks the rules,
Dutifully submits to the enchantment of type.

If each person has just one story to tell,
The self a Scheherazade postponing The End,
It's the friend alone who, night after night, listens,

His back to the camera, his expression now quizzical,
Now encouraging even though, because he has
A story himself, he's heard it all before.

III.

Is there such a thing as unrequited
Friendship? I doubt it. Even what's about
The house, as ordinary, as humble as habit—

The mutt, the TV, the rusted window tray
Of African violets in their tinfoil ruffs—
Returns our affection with a loyalty

Two parts pluck and the third a bright instinct
To please. (Our habits too are friends, of course.
The sloppy and aggressive ones as well

Seem pleas for attention from puberty's
Imaginary comrade or the Job's comforters
Of middle age.) Office mates or children

Don't form bonds but are merely busy together,
And acquaintances—that pen pal from Porlock is one—
Slip between the hours. But those we eagerly

Pursue bedevil the clock's idle hands,
And years later, by then the best of friends,
You'll settle into a sort of comfy marriage,

The two of you familiar as an old pair of socks,
Each darning the other with faint praise.
More easily mapped than kept to, friendships

Can stray, and who has not taken a wrong turn?
(Nor later put that misstep to good use.)
Ex-friends, dead friends, friends never made but missed,

How they resemble those shrouded chandeliers
Still hanging, embarrassed, noble, in the old palace
Now a state-run district conference center.

One peevish delegate is sitting there
Tapping his earphones because he's picking up
Static that sounds almost like trembling crystal.

IV.

Most friendships in New York are telephonic,
The actual meetings—the brunch or gallery hop
Or, best, a double-feature of French classics—

Less important than the daily schmooze.
Flopped on the sofa in my drip-dry kimono,
I kick off the morning's dance of hours with you,

Natalie, doyenne of the daily calls,
Master-mistress of crisis and charm.
Contentedly we chew the cud of yesterday's

Running feud with what part of the self
Had been mistaken—yes?—for someone else.
And grunt. Or laugh. Or leave to stir the stew.

Then talk behind the world's back—how, say,
Those friends of friends simply Will Not Do,
While gingerly stepping back (as we never would

With lover or stranger) from any disappointment
In each other. Grooming like baboons? Perhaps.
Or taking on a ballast of gossip to steady

Nerves already bobbing in the wake of that grand
Liner, the SS *Domesticity,*
With its ghost crew and endless fire drills.

But isn't the point to get a few things
Clear at last, some uncommon sense to rely
Upon in all this slow-motion vertigo

That lumbers from dream to real-life drama?
You alone, dear heart, remember what it's like
To be me; remember too the dollop of truth,

Cheating on that regime of artificially
Sweetened, salt-free fictions the dangerous
Years concoct for tonight's floating island.

V.

Different friends sound different registers.
The morning impromptu, when replayed this afternoon
For you, Jimmy, will have been transcribed

For downtown argot, oltrano, and Irish harp,
And the novelist in you draw out as anecdote
What news from nowhere had earlier surfaced as whim.

On your end of the line (I picture a fire laid
And high-tech teapot under a gingham cozy),
Patience humors my warmed-over grievance or gush.

Each adds the lover's past to his own, experience
Greedily annexed, heartland by buffer state,
While the friend lends his field glasses to survey

The ransacked loot and spot the weak defenses.
Though it believes all things, it's not love
That bears and hopes and endures, but the comrade-in-arms.

How often you've found me abandoned on your doormat,
Pleading to be taken in and plied
With seltzer and Chinese take-out, while you bandaged

My psyche's melodramatically slashed wrists
(In any case two superficial wounds),
The razor's edge of romance having fallen

Onto the bathroom tiles next to a lurid
Pool of self-regard. *"Basta!* Love
Would bake its bread of you, then butter it.

The braver remedy for sorrow is to stand up
Under fire, or lie low on a therapist's couch,
Whistling an old barcarole into the dark.

Get a grip. Buckle on your parachute.
Now, out the door with you, and just remember:
A friend in need is fortune's darling indeed."

VI.

Subtle Plato, patron saint of friendship,
Scolded those nurslings of the myrtle-bed
Whose tender souls, first seized by love's madness,

Then stirred to rapturous frenzies, overnight
Turn sour, their eyes narrowed with suspicions,
Sleepless, feverishly refusing company.

The soul, in constant motion because immortal,
Again and again is "deeply moved" and flies
To a new favorite, patrolling the upper air

To settle briefly on this or that heart-
Stopping beauty, or flutters vainly around
The flame of its own image, light of its life.

Better the friend to whom we're drawn by choice
And not instinct or the glass threads of passion.
Better the friend with whom we fall in step

Behind our proper god, or sit beside
At the riverbend, idly running a finger
Along his forearm when the conversation turns

To whether everything craves its opposite,
As cold its warmth and bitter its honeydrop,
Or whether like desires like—agreed?—

Its object akin to the good, recognizing
In another what is necessary for the self,
As one may be a friend without knowing how

To define friendship, which itself so often slips
Through our hands because . . . but he's asleep
On your shoulder by now and probably dreaming

Of a face he'd glimpsed on the street yesterday,
The stranger he has no idea will grow irreplaceable
And with whom he hasn't yet exchanged a word.

VII.

Late one night, alone in bed, the book
Having slipped from my hands while I stared at the phrase
The lover's plaintive "Can't we just be friends?"

I must have dreamt you'd come back, and sat down
Beside my pillow. (I could also see myself
Asleep but in a different room by now—

A motel room to judge by the landscape I'd become,
Framed on the cinder-block wall behind.)
To start over, you were saying, requires too much,

And friendship in the aftermath is a dull
Affair, a rendezvous with second guesses,
Dining out on memories you can't send back

Because they've spoiled. And from where I sat,
Slumped like a cloud over the moon's tabletop,
Its wrinkled linen trailing across a lake,

I was worried. Another storm was brewing.
I ran a willowy hand over the lake to calm
The moonlight—or your feelings. Then woke

On the bed's empty side, the sheets as cool
As silence to my touch. The speechlessness
Of sex, or the fumble afterwards for something

To say about love, amount to the same. Words
Are what friends, not lovers, have between them,
Old saws and eloquent squawkings. We deceive

Our lovers by falling for someone we cannot love,
Then murmur sweet nothings we do not mean,
Half-fearing they'll turn out true. But to go back—

Come dawn, exhausted by the quiet dark,
I longed for the paper boy's shuffle on the stair,
The traffic report, the voices out there, out there.

VIII.

Friends are fables of our loneliness.
If love would live for hope, friendship thrives
On memory, the friends we "make" made up

Of old desires for surprise without danger,
For support without a parent's smarting ruler,
For a brother's sweaty hand and a trail of crumbs.

Disguised in a borrowed cloak and hood, Christine
Has escaped with Octave the muddle of romance.
It is midnight. They are in the greenhouse, alone

But spied upon by jealousies that mistake
Anxiety for love, the crime that requires
An accomplice. Then, for no reason, *they* mistake

Themselves, and suddenly confess—the twin
Armed guards, Wish and Censor, having fallen
Asleep—to a buried passion for each other.

The friendship shudders. In the end, as if he's pushed
Christine toward a propeller blade for the pleasure
Of saving her, he sends the proper hero

In his place to meet her. His head still in the clouds,
The aviator races to his death, shot down
Like a pheasant the beaters had scared up for the hunt.

Christine, when she discovers the body, faints.
Her husband, the mooncalf cuckold, so that the game
Might continue, acts the gentleman, and thereby

Turns out the truest friend. He understands,
Is shaken but shrugs, and gracefully explains
"There's been the most deplorable accident . . ."

One guest begins to snigger in disbelief.
The old general defends his host: "The man has class.
A rare thing, that. His kind are dying out."

IX.

And when at last the lights come up, the echo
Of small arms fire on the soundtrack nextdoor
Ricochets into our multiplex cubicle.

Retreating up the empty aisle—the toss
Is heads for home, tails for ethnic out—
We settle on the corner sushi bar,

Scene of so many other films rehashed,
Scores retouched, minor roles recast,
Original endings restored or, better, rewritten,

So the stars up there will know what the two of us,
Seated in the dark, have come to learn
After all these years. How many is it now?

Twenty? Two hundred? Was it in high school or college
We met? The Film Society's aficionados-
Only, one-time, late-night *Rules of the Game,*

Wasn't it? By now even the classics
(Try that tuna epaulet) show their age,
Their breakneck rhythms gone off, their plots creaky.

But reflections our own first feathery daydreams
Cast on them still shimmer, and who looks back,
Airily, is a younger self, heedless

Of the cost to come, of love's fatal laws
Whose permanent suffering his joy postpones.
He's a friend too. But not so close as you.

He hasn't the taste for flaws that you and I
Share, and wants to believe in vice and genius,
The sort of steam that vanishes now above one

Last cup of tea—though I could sit here forever
Passing the life and times back and forth
Across the table with you, my ideal friend.

THE WINDOW

Even during the war, I used to get up at noon. The weariness—a damp, musky, still warm mold of myself—stayed in bed while I made coffee. If an idea disturbed this first surface of the day—like one of those tiny whirlpools that form the closer you come to the falls—it was easily ignored. I'd stand at the window in my underwear and blow on my cup and watch them drink in the café across the square. Afternoons, I'd sit in the back of the cinema, smoking, as sad and useless as a god. Long, crumpled nylons of cigarette smoke would drift up toward the projectionist's opening, then wrap around that single beam of romance from which, in those days, everything that counted came—the orphan on the train, the machine guns and lipstick, the water ballet, the ambush in the hotel corridor. When did it start? The moment you raised your arm to wave to someone across the street? The day you didn't answer the telephone and showed up later with your hair mussed? It wasn't until the war ended and the men came home that they too realized what had happened. By then they had lived so long in the hills and cellars and hardened themselves against regret that they hadn't the energy to retrieve any delicacy of feeling. Some bought that cheap religion, love, until they had no more belief to spend. Others tried the commonplace left out of their dreams: they made their beds in the morning and washed with plenty of soap, or stood round after round of drinks at the café, or counted on their children like the new government. Myself, I had my old habits, the letters to write to M., my diary, the dog. My train back—was it as long as a year ago now?—followed the shoreline by night. I could see little fires in the distance, and the moon laid like a compress on what beach the tide was giving up. By dawn the steam was settling on the fields. The tree-curtains parted to show a house on the crest of the hill, a lemon grove metallic against the blue sky, and then, closer, bullet-pocked, the red brick wall of a farm stable. The woman beside me had awakened by then, and asked me to help her with the window. It is easy to be good when you're not in love. You do someone a favor, and how soon you come to hate her grateful, radiant face.

after Pavese

KILIM

I.

The force of habit takes order to its heart,
As when a nurse, her basket filled with the dead
Child's toys, has put it by the head
Of her tomb, unwittingly on an acanthus root.

Kallimachos, they say, made his capital
Of it, when around that basket the thorny leaf
Sprang up, nature pressed down by grief
Into shapes that made the loss a parable,

His idea to change the shallow bead and reel
For an imprint of afterlife apparent to all,
Bringing down to earth an extravagance.

So skill gives way to art, or a headstone
To history—the body by now left alone,
As if bodies were the soul's ornaments.

II.

As if bodies were the soul's ornaments,
A mullah turned the Koran's carpet page.
Old Babur made a couplet instead—of Age
And Youth, his "throneless days," their violence.

The opium pearl, to ease him out of life,
Made a garden of pain. The rugs, the tent
Dissolved. A flower stall appeared. He went
On rearranging the couplet and devised,

To keep death at bay, five hundred and four
Versions. His first poem had been to a boy
From the bazaar whom for a day he had adored,

Whose glances he could still see in the dark
That lined the geometric border's void,
Reproduced in glistening egg-and-dart.

III.

Reproduction's glistening egg-and-dart,
Column or carpet, whatever cultures may rest
Upon, and couples do, like Prussian drill . . .
Nietzsche said the poem is a dance
In chains. Molecular life enchained by chance?
The bonds of atoms formulas distill
Are strains that resonate, the elements
Held both far together and close apart.

The rose window, its creation story speechless,
Its pattern telling all, duplicates
The cross-sectioned axial view each strand
Of genetic coil reveals. Each grain of sand
Takes an eternity to articulate
History's figure of speech for randomness.

IV.

History's figures of speech for randomness—
    Car-bomb, rape, skyjack, carcinogens,
    Dragon's teeth sown in the morning headlines,

    Blips on a monitor, all this summer's kinds
    Of long-festering terrorist violence
A final demand, its victims slumped, helpless—

How muffled they seem in my own bloodstream,
    And here in Vermont, whose coldhearted self
        Has long gone underground. The daydream
Of a hooded finch on the thistle's globe. The stealth

Of mallow colonizing clapboard. The beard
        And turban on one last old iris. Who knows
    If the image also frees what it's commandeered.
Meaning's subversive, being superimposed.

V.

Meaning, subversive because superimposed,
Signs on a dotted line of brushwood its truce,
Its terms with mountains out beyond my window's

Squaring off with cloudspray, a crest of spruce,
The green, landlocked swell and trough this state
Navigates, a chaos first unloosed

In the crown glass whose own wavering is bated
Breath upon the waters, then onto the wide
Pine floor of my study and the kilim—ornate

But frayed—that has designs on it. As if I'd
Come ashore and a moon been brought to light
The new world's passageways, its thread inside

The carpet's magic, I hear something like
So strangely silent this still desert night . . .

VI.

so   strangely silent   this still desert night
you kneel on me to pray   lanternlight

rows of petalled guls   to guard the borders
his knot garden opposite the women's quarters

nomad bands   a running dog   four split
leaf lobed medallions   concentric

threats   dollar signs   God is everywhere
a janissary comet   the mihrab's stair

and doorway   the prophet's place in his house
a sura the flame flickers on as if in doubt

the strain on paradise in its descent
hollowed out the moon jangles   the tent

pole sways   look   the heart slows
a wind that frames and fills the scene   O rose

VII.

The wind that frames and fills the scene arose
Between the mountains and the nomad camp,
Grazing the flocks, their pile of wool that combs
Had plied for spinning like stories still damp

With last night's storm of raw material,
The strands to be drawn into the spindle's plot,
Tightening for the warp, but nearly all
The weft yarn as loosely spun as thought.

Saffron, indigo, and cochineal,
The pots of dye have simmered through the night.
The loom is ready. Dawn sits by the fields
To stir. All color is an effect of light.

The woman dreams of patterns the sky might yield,
Of love's unchanging aspect in starlight.

VIII.

And love's unchanging aspect—by starlight
    Whose cressets are blurred
  In the brazier's perfumed smoke,
A bride enters her husband's tent, her birthright
    And dowry now spread or stowed
As he sees fit, and later a child whose first
Toy is a shuttle—watches over her work.

She weaves the carpet from memory, a talent
    Her hands recollect,
  Though bound to a narrow loom
As to the tribe's own wayworn valley,
    Its tripod stakes festooned
With skeins of past and future their lives connect
When seen and heard in the fabric's page of text.

IX.

When seen and heard as one, a page of text
    And an urgent voice make up a history—
Matter, pattern, sources a poem selects.
    The carpet, too, is a complicity.
When grown at ten, the child may sit beside
    The other women and in time betray
Her mother's hand, the seed pods multiplied
    On a blank expanse, in favor of her father's way
With zigzag diagonals (he had seen
    The electric plant at Shiraz) and a few of her own
        Imaginings. By twenty she'll have learned
To read. Hafiz says love is never free
    Of choice. The rose's tongues, or its thorn alone.
    A palm-read pool, or its vacillating pattern.

X.

A palm. A red pool. The vacillating pattern
Of television lights on the bloodslick.
The diplomat still seated. The powder burn
On his neck like a new neighborhood picked

Out by rocket fire from the Shuf. A note,
A warning from Hezbollah, pinned to his shirt.
The day before, ten children had almost
Escaped a mortar. How much death will serve?

The assassin's mother and her mother's mother
Wove carpets. Now the time for art is past.
There is no god but God. To be a martyr
Is both thread and legend. The pistol gives her wrist
The graveside ache that, as her father's mourner,
The first stone she tossed created. And the next.

XI.

The touchstone I toss first creates but next
(Because the poem always has a shadow
Under its reliefs, unlike a carpet's
Flat entanglements, its straight and narrow
Life without illusions, turned inward
Like a dream, or like that disinterred
Necropolis Beirut's become of late—
The savagery of the abstract, form or faith—
And because that shadow is the natural world
The poem's grounded in and the figures branching
Up from it, like an oasis to the approaching
Caravan lost and found in a blinding swirl
Of sand, the mirage they drink in before they turn)
Disrupts. The way things go we come to learn.

XII.

Disrupting the way things go, we come to learn,
Informs the art. Weavers incorporate
A flaw, the stitch dropped or badly turned,
To remind who kneel that only God is great,
Perfection His, His the privilege to create.
And on the block we guard or square we thread,
If thought is our element—a fiery hate,
A patient air, the earth we defend and dread—
Its flaw is the very idea that, above or ahead,
Perfection exists, the god hidden in habit.

She wakes in pain, the night cut down, her bed
A dirt floor—but there's the sun, and the stab it
Makes behind her eyes. The day's at hand.
A light signals from the mountains now, as planned.

XIII.

Some light is on the mountains now. A plan
Of the city taped to her wall, the day's targets
Marked, a red inaudible word on each . . .
A band of sun edges up on that paper too.
The grid of streets, the harbor's selvage, the mosques
And prismatic parks, the quadrants colored by faction,
When brought to such a light take on a kilim's
Dispositions.
              No art can stop the killings,
Nor any point of view make an abstraction
Of the child murdered because a boundary was crossed.
The living and the dead are woven through
Us, back and forth, in and out of my speech—
The bullets' stammer, the longest threads in the carpet—
As if everything she knows I understand.

XIV.

As if everything we've known we understand,
A deal is struck. The familiar guarantee—
That for his trouble the buyer may demand
The weaver have gone blind to finish the work—
Applies. A hookah is brought. A glass of tea.
And what we've bargained for is something framed,
As night by day, an anarchy on which, alert
To lives now lost in thought, the eye is trained.

Correspondences in camouflage.
Reflected in the windowpane, we pay attention
To each in turn, the pieces of a world dislodged—
Beirut, Vermont, the surfaces that start
To yield, and depths that hold their breath, a tension
The force of habit takes as order to the heart.

XV.

The force of habit's taken order to its heart,
As if bodies were the soul's ornaments,
Reproduction's glistening egg-and-dart.
History's figures of speech for randomness—
Meaning subversive because superimposed—
Are so strangely silent this still desert night
That a wind to frame and fill the scene arose,
And love's changing aspect in starlight
We can see and hear as a single page of text,
A palm-read pool whose vacillating pattern
The touchstone I toss first creates but next
Disrupts. The way things go we come to learn.
    A light is on the mountains now, as planned,
    As if everything we've known we understand.

from TEN COMMANDMENTS

1998

THE LEDGER

Love is injustice, said Camus.
We want to be loved. What's still more true?
Each wants most to be preferred,
And listens for those redeeming words
Better than X, more than Y—
Enough to quiet the child's cry,
The bridegroom's nerves, the patient's
Reluctant belief in providence.
Break what you can, hurt whom you will,
Humiliate the others until
Someone takes a long, hard look.
Oh Love, put down your balance book.

MY SIDESHOW

Summers during the Eisenhower years, a carnival
Came to town. From my father's pair of bleacher seats,
The safety net under the Big Top's star attractions,
The drugged tiger, the stilted clowns, the farting scooters
All seemed as little death-defying as those routines
The high-wire trio staged with their jerky parasols.

With that singular lack of shame only a kid commands,
I'd sneak over instead to the sawdusted sideshow tent.
Every year *they* were back: the fire-breathing women,
The men who swallowed scimitars or hammered nails
Up their noses and fishhooks through their tongues,
The dwarf in his rayon jockstrap and sequined sweatband.

A buck got you into the blow-off where a taped grind
Spieled the World of Wonders while a blanket rose
On seven clear ten-gallon jars that held
Pickled fetuses—real or rubber?—their limbs
Like ampersands, each with something deliriously wrong,
Too little of this in front or too much of that behind.

Four-legged chickens, a two-headed raccoon,
The Mule-Faced Girl, the Man with Four Pupils
In His Eyes, coffined devil babies, the Penguin Boy,
The Living Skeleton, an avuncular thousand-pound
Sort who swilled cans of soda and belched at us. . . .
What I think of the Word Made Flesh developed in this darkroom.

Back then I couldn't wait for hair to appear on my face
And down below, where my flashlight scrutinized at bedtime.
I'd rise and fall by chance, at the table, on buses, in class.
My voice cracked. I was shooting up and all thumbs.
Oh, the restless embarrassments of late childhood!
My first pimple—huge and lurid—had found its place.

I kept staring at one jar. The thing inside seemed to float
Up from a fishtail that was either leg or penis—or both.
(I could hear my father now, outside the tent, calling me.)
From its mouth, a pair of delicate legs emerged,
As if it had swallowed a perfect twin. I gulped. Something
Unspoken, then and since, rose like acid in my throat.

MY EARLY HEARTS

The over-crayoned valentine FOЯ MOTHEЯ.
   The furtive gym-class crush.
In my missal the polychrome Sacred Heart
   Our Savior exposes,
The emblems of his Passion still festering,
   The knotted scourge, the sponge,
The nailhead studs all sweating blood from inside
   A little crown of thorns
Tightening around my groin as I pulled back
   The crushed-velvet curtain
And entered the confessional's dark chamber.
   Whatever lump in the throat
Aztec horror tales had once contrived to raise
   Melted in the aftermath
Of eating—myself both high priest and victim
   On his knees, head yanked back—
The live, quivering heart of thwarted romance,
   A taste one swallowed hard
First to acquire, and much later to mock.
   Hearts bid on, hearts broken.
The shape of a flame reversed in the Zippo
   Cupped close to light one last
Cigarette before walking out on a future.
   The shape two fat, rain-soaked
Paperbacks assumed on the back-porch table
   After I'd left for home,
That whole summer spent reading Tolstoy, sleeping
   With my window open
Onto an imaginary grove of birch—
   One of which I had carved
Two names on and sat under with my diary
   To watch the harvesting.

There is a black heart somewhere—the clarinet
    In K. 581,
Still aching for the pond edge, the rippling pain,
    The god's quick grasp of things.
A white one, too—that teardrop pearl on Vermeer's
    Girl at the Frick, hanging
Above her interrupted letter, mirror
    To what she's left unsaid.

At ten, on a grade-school excursion downtown
    To the science museum,
I learned my lesson once and for all—how to
    Lose myself in a heart.
In that case, a cavernous, walk-through model
    With narrow, underlit
Arterial corridors and piped-in thumps.
    As so often later,
The blindfold loosely fastened by loneliness
    Seemed to help me stumble
Past the smeary diagrams and push-button
    Explanations, helped me
Ignore the back-of-the-closet, sour-milk
    Smells and the silly jokes
Of classmates in the two-storey lung next door.
    For those others, the point
Was to end up only where they had begun,
    Back at the start of something,
Eager for the next do-it-yourself gadget.
    I stayed behind, inside,
Under the mixed blessing of not being missed.
    I could hear the old nun
Scolding some horseplay, more faintly leading them
    On to a further room,
"Where a giant pendulum will simulate

The crisscrossed Sands of Time. . . ."
What had time to do with anything *I* wanted!
    At last I had the heart
All to myself, my name echoing through it
    As I called to myself
In a stage whisper from room to blood-red room.
    And what of the smaller,
Racing heart—my own, that is—inside the heart
    Whose very emptiness
Had by now come to seem a sort of shelter?
    Was it—*me,* I mean, *my* heart—
Even back then ready to stake everything,
    To endure the trials
By fire and water, to pledge long silence,
    Accept the surprises
And sad discoveries one loses his way
    Among, walking around
And around his own heart, looking for a way
    That leads both in and out?

It happens first in one's own heart, doesn't it?
    And then in another's.
Something happens when you hear it happening.
    One day, out of the blue,
An old friend shows up and needs, so you'd thought, just
    A shoulder to cry on.
Or a new friend is stirring in the next room.
    Or the stranger in bed
Beside you gets up in the middle of the night.
    You listen for the steps.
Unfamiliar steps are coming closer, close
    Enough to reach out for.
Come over here, love. Bend down and put your head
    To my chest. Now listen.

Listen. Do you hear them? After all this time
    There are your own footsteps.
Can you hear yourself walking toward me now?

MY OLD IDOLS

I. *At Ten*

1955. A scratchy waltz
Buzzed over the ice rink's P.A.
My classmate Tony, the barber's son: "Alls
He wantsa do is, you know, like, play."

Bored with perfecting my languid figure eights,
I trailed him to a basement door marked GENTS
With its metal silhouette of high-laced skates
(Symbols, I guess, of methods desire invents).

Tony's older brother was waiting inside.
I'd been "requested," it seemed. He was sixteen,
Tall, rawboned, blue-eyed,
Thumbs hooked into faded, tightening jeans.

I fumbled with small talk, pretending to be shy.
Looking past me, he slowly unzipped his fly.

II. *Callas*

Her voice: steeped in a rancid clotting syrup:
Whatever's not believed remains a grace
While again she invokes the power that yields:
Splintered timber and quick consuming flame:
The simplest way to take hold of the heart's
Complications, its pool of spilt religion:
A long black hair sweat-stuck to the skin:
The bitter sleep of the dying: the Jew in Berlin:

Who sent you here? the sharp blade pleads:
Stormcloud: thornhedge: starchill:
Blood bubble floating to the top of the glass:
The light, from fleshrise to soulset:
The world dragging the slow weight of its shame
Like the train of pomp: guttering candle: her voice.

III. In Class

Parasangs, satraps, the daily drill . . .
Beginner's Greek its own touchstone.
The sophomore teacher was Father Moan,
Whom I longed to have praise my skill.
The illustrated reader's best
Accounts of murder and sacrifice
Only suggested the heavy price
I longed to pay at his behest.

He'd slap the pointer against his thigh.
I quivered. What coldness may construe
Of devotion was an experience
As hard to learn as catch his eye.
I kept my hand up. *Here!* I knew
The right answer. The case. The tense.

MY MAMMOGRAM

I.

In the shower, at the shaving mirror or beach,
For years I'd led . . . the unexamined life?
When all along and so easily within reach
(Closer even than the nonexistent wife)

Lay the trouble—naturally enough
Lurking in a useless, overlooked
Mass of fat and old newspaper stuff
About matters I regularly mistook

As a horror story for the opposite sex,
Nothing to do with what at my downtown gym
Are furtively ogled as The Guy's Pecs.

But one side is swollen, the too tender skin
Discolored. So the doctor orders an X-
Ray, and nervously frowns at my nervous grin.

II.

Mammography's on the basement floor.
The nurse has an executioner's gentle eyes.
I start to unbutton my shirt. She shuts the door.
Fifty, male, already embarrassed by the size

Of my "breasts," I'm told to put the left one
Up on a smudged, cold, Plexiglas shelf,
Part of a robot half menacing, half glum,
Like a three-dimensional model of the Freudian self.

Angles are calculated. The computer beeps.
Saucers close on a flatness further compressed.
There's an ache near the heart neither dull nor sharp.

The room gets lethal. Casually the nurse retreats
Behind her shield. Anxiety as blithely suggests
I joke about a snapshot for my Christmas card.

III.

"No sign of cancer," the radiologist swans
In to say—with just a hint in his tone
That he's done me a personal favor—whereupon
His look darkens. "But what these pictures show . . .

Here, look, you'll notice the gland on the left's
Enlarged. See?" I see an aerial shot
Of Iraq, and nod. "We'll need further tests,
Of course, but I'd bet that what *you've* got

Is a liver problem. Trouble with your estrogen
Levels. It's time, my friend, to take stock.
It happens more often than you'd think to men."

Reeling from its millionth scotch on the rocks,
In other words, my liver's sensed the end.
Why does it come as something less than a shock?

IV.

The end of life as I've known it, that is to say—
Testosterone sported like a power tie,
The matching set of drives and dreads that may
Now soon be plumped to whatever new designs

My apparently resentful, androgynous
Inner life has on me. Blind seer?
The Bearded Lady in some provincial circus?
Something that others both desire and fear.

Still, doesn't everyone *long* to be changed,
Transformed to, no matter, a higher or lower state,
To know the leathery D-Day hero's strange

Detachment, the queen bee's dreamy loll?
Yes, but the future each of us blankly awaits
Was long ago written on the genetic wall.

V.

So suppose the breasts fill out until I look
Like my own mother . . . ready to nurse a son,
A version of myself, the infant understood
In the end as the way my own death had come.

Or will I in a decade be back here again,
The diagnosis this time not freakish but fatal?
The changes in one's later years all tend,
Until the last one, toward the farcical,

Each of us slowly turned into something that hurts,
Someone we no longer recognize.
If soul is the final shape I shall assume,

The shadow brightening against the fluorescent gloom,
An absence as clumsily slipped into as this shirt,
Then which of my bodies will have been the best disguise?

FOUND PARABLE

In the men's room at the office today
some wag has labelled the two stalls
    the *Erotic* and the *Political*.
The second seems suitable for the results
of my business, not for what thinking
    ordinarily accompanies it.
So I've locked myself into the first because,
though farther from the lightbulb overhead,
    it remains the more conventional
and thereby illuminating choice.
The wit on its walls is more desperate.
    As if I had written them
there myself, but only because by now
I have seen them day after day,
    I know each boast, each plea,
the runty widower's resentments,
the phone number for good head.
    Today's fresh drawing:
a woman's torso, neck to outflung knees,
with breasts like targets and at her crotch
    red felt-tip "hair" to guard
a treasure half wound, half wisecrack.
The first critic of the flesh is always
    the self-possessed sensualist.
With all that wall as his margin,
he had sniffed in smug ballpoint
    OBVIOUSLY DONE BY SOMEONE
WHO HAS NEVER SEEN THE REAL THING.
Under that, in a later hand,
    the local pinstripe aesthete
had dismissed the daydreamer's crudity
and its critic's edgy literalism.

His block letters had squared,
not sloping shoulders: NO,
BY SOMEONE WHO JUST CAN'T DRAW.
　　Were the two opinions
converging on the same moral point?
That a good drawing *is* the real thing?
　　Or that the real thing
can be truly seen only through another's
eyes? But now that I trace it through
　　other jokes and members,
the bottom line leads to a higher inch
of free space on the partition—
　　a perch above the loose
remarks, like the pimp's doorway
or the Zen master's cliff-face ledge.
　　THERE ARE NO REAL THINGS
writes the philosopher. But he too
has been misled by everything
　　the mind makes of a body.
When the torso is fleshed out
and turns over in the artist's bed,
　　when the sensualist sobs over her,
when the critic buttons his pants,
when the philosopher's scorn sinks back
　　from a gratified ecstasy,
then it will be clear to each
in his own way. There is nothing
　　we cannot possibly not know.

TEA WITH THE LOCAL SAINT

I'd bought a cone of solid sugar and a box
Of tea for the saint himself, a flashlight
For his son, the saint-elect, and bubblegum
For a confusion of small fry—the five-year-old
Aunt, say, and her seven-year-old nephew.
Nothing for the women, of course, the tattooed,
One-eyed, moon-faced matron, or her daughter
Whose husband had long ago run away
After killing their newborn by pouring
A bottle of cheap cologne down its throat.
This was, after all, our first meeting.

I was to be introduced by a Peace Corps pal
Whose easy, open California ways
Had brought a water system to the village
And an up-to-date word to its vocabulary.
Every other guttural spillway of Arabic
Included a carefully enunciated "awesome,"
The speaker bright-eyed with his own banter.
We sat on a pair of Kurt Cobain beach towels
And under a High-Quality Quartz Clock,
The plastic butterflies attached to whose hands
Seemed to keep time with those in my stomach.

At last, he entered the room, the saint himself,
Moulay Madani, in a white head scarf and caftan
The fading blue of a map's Moroccan coastline,
Its hem embroidered with geometric ports of call.
A rugged sixty, with a longshoreman's jaw,
A courtier's guile, and a statesman's earnest pauses,
He first explained the crescent dagger he fingered
Had been made two centuries ago by a clever Jew.

Then he squinted for my reaction. I've no taste
For bad blood, and gingerly cleared my throat to say
I was inclined to trust any saint who carried a knife.

From a copper urn, glasses of mint tea were poured,
Of a tongue-stiffening sweetness. I was allowed to wave
Away the tray of nougat—or rather, the flies on it.
Sipping, I waited for a word, a sign from the saint.
I'd wanted to lie, as if underground, and watch
Him dig up the sky, or stand at a riverbank
And have the water sweep off my presumptions,
Have him blow light into my changeling bones.
I wanted to feel the stalk rise and the blade fall.
I wanted my life's arithmetic glazed and fired.
I wanted the hush, the wingstroke, the shudder.

But sainthood, I learned soon enough, is a fate
Worse than life, nights on call for the demons
In a vomiting lamb, a dry breast, a broken radio,
And days spent parroting the timeless adages,
Spent arbitrating water rights, property lines,
Or feuds between rival herdsmen over scrub brush,
Spent blessing every bride and anyone's big-bellied
Fourth or fifth wife, praying that they deliver sons.
I thought back to the time, not ten feet from him,
I heard a homily delivered by old John XXIII,
Sounding wholly seraphic in his murmured Italian.

Ten interpreters stepped from behind the throne.
The English one at last explained the Holy Father
Had urged us all to wear seatbelts while driving.
My heart sank at its plain good sense, as hymns
Echoed and golden canopies enfolded the pope.
How like home it seemed, with my own father

A preoccupied patriarch of practicality
When what was wanted veered wildly between
The gruff headmaster and the drunken playwright.
Instead, I got the distant advertising salesman,
The suburban dad of what turned out to be my dreams. . . .

Dreams that, decades later, back at my hotel in Fez,
A bucket of cold water was suddenly poured on.
I'd gone to the hamam, stripped, and lay on a pattern
Of sopping tiles that might have spelled God's will.
Steam shrouded the attendant methodically soaping
The knots of disappointment he'd knuckled in my back.
He paused. I drifted. [*Yowza!*] I looked up
At a bald, toothless gnome in swaddling clothes
On his way back to the fountain for more bad news.
Something in his bowlegged walk—perhaps the weary
Routine of it—made me think of the saint again,

Of how, when tea was done, and everyone had stood,
He reached for my head, put his hands over it,
And gently pulled me to his chest, which smelled
Of dung-smoke and cinnamon and mutton grease.
I could hear his wheezy breathing now, like the prophet's
Last whispered word repeated by the faithful.
Then he prayed for what no one had time to translate—
His son interrupted the old man to tell him a group
Of snake charmers sought his blessing, and a blind thief.
The saint pushed me away, took one long look,
Then straightened my collar and nodded me toward the door.

for Jane Garmey

UNDER HYDRA

To disbelieve in God—or worse, in His servants—
 Of old incited mobs
 With stones or stakes grimly to atone for what,
 Like a bomb not lobbed
But planted in the garage of a mirror-skin
 High-rise, has from deep within
 Too suddenly exposed
 The common desire to learn
 Less than had been supposed.

Bedsores, point shaving, a taste for sarongs. There are signs
 Everywhere—like the thumbprints,
 Say, of thin-lipped men or sluggish women
 On an heirloom violin.
So mine is the culture of laugh track and chat room.
 Authority's foredoomed.
 Where is distance, and what
 Can frighten or inspire, condemn or redeem?
 All transcendence is cut

With a canned, buttoned-down, fork-tongued coziness.
 The stars are hooded now.
 The heart's cloud chamber weeps its nuclear tears.
 My nails are bitten, and how
All-consuming my vanities, the fancied slights
 To my air-kissing appetites.
 Millennial echoes
 Fill the abandoned stadium. Homeless
 Frauds crowd the two back rows.

Compel them to come in, the evangelist
        Insists. There are empty
    Seats at the table for minims and ranters.
        Join the ancient family
Squabbles—whose is bigger? who deserves more?
        Prophecy's the trapdoor
        Whose fatal saving grace
    Leads to listening for a voice within
        That doubles as self-praise.

His lips cut off, and flames at work on his bubbling guts,
        The wandering monk is tied
    To his own refusal—a book or belief.
        The scholar, for his pride,
Is whipped, branded, and in midwinter sent out
        On the road of his doubt
        To perish of the cold.
    Judge and martyr each invokes God's mercy
        On his innocent soul.

There goes the pitiful procession of mumblers,
        Slave masters and skinheads,
    Witches, dealers, backwoods ayatollahs.
        And here am I, tucked in bed,
Wondering if I believe in anything more
        Than my devotions and four
        Squares. And if forced to say,
    Wouldn't I deny even you, love, for a future?
        Who spoke the truth today?

AUDEN'S OED

in the old oxblood edition, the color
   of the mother tongue, all foxed and forked,
its threadbare edges dented, once a fixture
   in the second-storey Kirchstetten
room where day by day he fashioned the silence
   into objects, often sitting on
Poy–Ry, say, or *Sole–Sz,* and after his death
   sent packing from cozy Austria
to Athens, where fortune dropped it from Chester's
   trembling hands into a legacy
that exiled it next to page-curling Key West
   and finally to Connecticut,
is shelved here now, a long arm's-length from my desk.
   What he made of himself he had found
in this book, the exact weight of each soft spot
   and sore point, how each casts a shadow
understudying our hungers and our whims.
   If history is just plain dull facts,
the facts are these, these ruling nouns and upstart
   verbs, these slick adjectival toadies
and adverbial agents with their collars
   pulled up, privileged phrasal moments,
and full-scale clausal changes that qualify
   or contradict the course of a life.
This book is all we can remember and dream.
   It's how spur gears mesh and rocks are parsed
into geodes, how the blood engorges
   a glance, how the fig ripens to fall,
or what quarter-tones and quarks may signal deep
   inside a precise idea of space.
It is to this book he sat for the lessons
   the past had set him—how our Greeks died,

whom your Romans killed, how her Germans
    overreached, what his English understood,
how my Americans denied history
    was anything but an innocence
the others had simply skimmed or mispronounced.
    He knew history is a grammar,
and grammar a metaphor, and poetry
    nothing more or less than death itself—
it never lies because it never affirms.
    From the start, squinting at the propped score
with Mother in their duets at the upright
    or biting his nails while arguing
the quidditas of thuggish jacks-in-office,
    he knew what he called truth always lies
in the words and so in this dictionary,
    which like him has become a conscience
with all its roots, all its ramifications,
    meanings and examples down the years.
It was on this book he sat for the lessons
    learned five inches above a desk chair,
five inches to lean down closer to the page,
    one volume at a time, day by day,
slightly above the sense of things, but closer
    to what tomorrow so many others
will consider to have somehow been the truth.

The hard part is not so much telling the truth
    as knowing which truth to tell—or worse,
what it is you want to tell the truth, and how
    at last one learns to unlove others,
to uncast the spells, to rewind the romance
    back to its original desire
for something else altogether, its grievance,
    say, against that year's dazzling head boy

or the crippled wide-eyed horse you couldn't shoot.
    And, as innocent as the future
porno star's first milk tooth, the dictionary
    has no morality other than
definition itself. The large, functional
    Indo-European family
will do for a murky myth of origin,
    and the iron laws of shift and change
go unquestioned by the puzzled rummager.
    Our names for things tend to hold them fast
in place, give an X its features or its pitch,
    a fourth dimension of distinctness.
And what may seem vague awaits the Supplement
    just now pulling into the depot,
late as usual but looming through the steam.
    Words have their unflappable habits
of being, constellations of fixed ideas
    that still move. Sentimentality,
Snobbery, Sympathy, Sorrow—each queues up
    at the same window. No raised eyebrow
for the faked orgasm or press conference
    to issue official denials.
No sigh for the botanist's crabbed notebook.
    No praise for the florilegium.
No regret for the sinking tanker's oil slick
    glittering now off Cape Flattery.
No truck with bandbox grooming, fashion runways,
    the foot binder's stale apology,
or the dream's down payment and layaway plan.
    Everything adds up to or sinks back
into the word we know it by in this book.
    A believer in words—common prayers
or textbook theories—this wrinkled metaphor
    of the mind itself abided by

what grave and lucid laws, what keen exemptions
    these columns of small print have upheld.
He could be sitting beside one, chin in hand,
    listening to a late quartet, a gaze
on his face only the final chord will break.
    Here is that faraway something else,
here between the crowded lines of scholarship.
    Here is the first rapture and final
dread of being found out by words, terms, phrases
    for what is unknown, unfelt, unloved.
Here in the end is the language of a life.

Half my life ago, before retiring
    to new digs under Oxford's old spires,
as a part of his farewell tour of the States,
    one last look at the rooms of the house
he'd made of our poised, mechanical largesse,
    he visited my alma mater.
The crowd—tweedy townies and student groundlings—
    packed the hall and spilled over the lawn
outside, where the lucky ones pressed their faces
    to windows suspense was steaming up.
How did I find a place at the master's feet?
    My view was of the great man's ankles,
and close enough to see his socks didn't match.
    I sat there uncomfortably but spellbound
to his oracular mumble. And later,
    after the applause and the sherry,
while he wambled tipsily toward his guest suite,
    I sprang as if by coincidence
from its darkened doorway where I'd been waiting.
    But, well, waiting for *what* exactly?
Suddenly speechless, I counted on a lie
    and told him I knew his work by heart

and would he autograph my unread copy.
    He reached in his jacket for a pen
and at last looked distractedly up at me.
    A pause. "Turn around and bend over,"
he ordered in a voice vexed with impatience
    I at once mistook for genuine
interest—almost a proposition, in fact.
    The coy young man I was then is not
my type, but I can recognize the appeal.
    Even as I wheeled slowly around
and put my hands on my knees, I realized
    what he wanted, what he'd asked of me.
To write in the book, he required a desk.
    My back would do as well as any
Tree trunk or cafeteria tabletop.
    Only years later did it make sense.
By then I'd figured out that he'd been writing
    on me ever since that encounter,
or that I'd unconsciously made of myself
    a desk so that he could continue—
the common imagination's dogsbody
    and ringmaster—still to speak up,
however halting or indirect the voice.

Today, sitting down at six to darn the day
    with a drink, I glanced across the room
to my desk, where Wystan, my month-old tabby,
    lay asleep on an open volume
of the wizard's unfailing dictionary,
    faultless creaturely Instinct atwitch
on a monument. How to sneak out past him
    for the sweating martini shaker?
My clumsy tiptoe prompts a faint annoyance—
    a single eye unlidded, a yawn,

his right paw, claws outstretched, pointing to *soodle*.
    Weren't these—the cat and book, or instinct
and idea—the two angels on his shoulder?
    Together, they'd made him suspicious
of the holy crusade, the top of the charts,
    compulsive hygiene, debt, middlemen,
seaside cottages, crooners, Gallic charm,
    public charities, the forgeries
of statecraft, the fantasies of the bedroom,
    easy assumptions, and sweeping views.
The kitten's claws have somehow caught in the page
    and puckered it so that, skewed sideways,
it resembles—or rather, for the moment
    I can make out in the lines of type—
the too often folded map his face looked like.
    Protect me, St. Wiz, protect us all
from this century by your true example.
    With what our language has come to know
about us, protect us still from both how much
    and how little we can understand
ourselves, from the unutterable blank page
    of soul, from the echoing silence
moments after the heavy book is slammed shut.

WHAT THEY LEFT BEHIND

The room with double beds, side by side.
One was the bed of roses, still made up,
The other the bed of nails, all undone.
In the nightstand clamshell, two Marlboro butts.

On the shag, a condom with a tear in its tip
Neither of them noticed—or would even suspect
For two years more. A ballpoint embossed
By a client's firm: Malpractice Suits.

A wad of gum balled in a page of proverbs
Torn from the complimentary Bible.
His lipstick. Her aftershave.

A dream they found the next day they'd shared:
All the dogs on the island were dying
And the birds had flown up into the lonely air.

PROUST IN BED

Through the peephole he could see a boy
Playing patience on the huge crimson sofa.
    There was the carpet, the second-best
Chairs, the old chipped washstand, all his dead parents'
        Things donated months ago
        "To make an unfortunate
        Crowd happy" at the Hôtel
        Marigny, Albert's brothel,
Warehouse of desires
And useless fictions—

For one of which he turned to Albert
And nodded, he'd have that one at cards, the soon-
    To-be footman or fancy butcher.
He'd rehearsed his questions in the corridor.
        Did you kill an animal
        Today? An ox? Did it bleed?
        Did you touch the blood? Show me
        Your hands, let me see how you . . .
(Judgment Day angel
Here to separate

The Good from the Bad, to weigh the soul . . .
Soon enough you'll fall from grace and be nicknamed
    Pamela the Enchantress or Tool
Of the Trade. Silliness is the soul's sweetmeat.)
        One after another now,
        Doors closed on men in bed with
        The past, it was three flights to
        His room, the bedroom at last,
The goal obtained and
So a starting point

For the next forbidden fruit—the taste
Of apricots and ripe gruyère is on the hand
   He licks—the next wide-open mouth
To slip his tongue into like a communion
        Wafer. The consolation
        Of martyrs is that the God
      For whom they suffer will see
      Their wounds, their wildernesses.
He's pulled a fresh sheet
Up over himself,

   As if waiting for his goodnight kiss
While the naked boy performs what he once did
   For himself. It's only suffering
Can make us all more than brutes, the way that boy
        Suffers the silvery thread
        To be spun inside himself,
      The snail track left on lilac,
      Its lustrous mirror-writing,
The mysterious
Laws drawn through our lives

   Like a mother's hand through her son's hair . . .
But again nothing comes of it. The signal
   Must be given, the small bedside bell.
He needs his parents to engender himself,
        To worship his own body
        As he watches them adore
      Each other's. The two cages
      Are brought in like the holy
Sacrament. Slowly
The boy unveils them.

The votive gaslights seem to flicker.
Her dying words were "What have you done to me?"
In each cage a rat, and each rat starved
For three days, each rat furiously circling
The pain of its own hunger.
Side by side the two cages
Are placed on the bed, the foot
Of the bed, right on the sheet
Where he can see them
Down the length of his

Body, helpless now as it waits there.
The rats' angry squealing sounds so far away.
He looks up at his mother—touches
Himself—at her photograph on the dresser,
His mother in her choker
And her heavy silver frame.
The tiny wire-mesh trapdoors
Slide open. At once the rats
Leap at each other,
Claws, teeth, the little

Shrieks, the flesh torn, torn desperately,
Blood spurting out everywhere, hair matted, eyes
Blinded with the blood. Whichever stops
To eat is further torn. The half-eaten rat
Left alive in the silver
Cage the boy—he keeps touching
Himself—will stick over and
Over with a long hatpin.
Between his fingers
He holds the pearl drop.

She leans down over the bed, her veil
Half-lifted, the scent of lilac on her glove.
His father hates her coming to him
Like this, hates her kissing him at night like this.

THREE DREAMS ABOUT ELIZABETH BISHOP

I.

It turned out the funeral had been delayed a year.
The casket now stood in the state capitol rotunda,
An open casket. You lay there like Lenin
Under glass, powdered, in powder blue
But crestfallen, if that's the word
For those sagging muscles that make the dead
Look grumpy. The room smelled of gardenias.
Or no, I *was* a gardenia, part of a wreath
Sent by the Radcliffe Institute and right behind
You, with a view down the line of mourners.
When Lloyd and Frank arrived, both of them
Weeping and reciting—was it "Thanatopsis"?—
A line from Frank about being the brother
To a sluggish clod was enough to wake you up.
One eye, then the other, slowly opened.
You didn't say anything, didn't have to.
You just blinked, or I did, and in another room
A group of us sat around your coffin chatting.
Once in a while you would add a comment—
That, no, hay was stacked with beaverslides,
And, yes, it was a blue, a mimeograph blue
Powder the Indians used, and stuck cedar pegs
Through their breasts in the ghost dance—
All this very slowly. Such an effort for you
To speak, as if underwater and each bubble-
Syllable had to be exhaled, leisurely
Floated up to the surface of our patience.
Still alive, days later, still laid out
In a party dress prinked with sun sparks,

Hands folded demurely across your stomach,
You lay on the back lawn, uncoffined,
Surrounded by beds of freckled foxglove
And fool-the-eye lilies that only last a day.
By then Lowell had arrived, young again
But shaggy even in his seersucker and tie.
He lay down alongside you to talk.
The pleasure of it showed in your eyes,
Widening, then fluttering with the gossip,
Though, of course, you still didn't move at all,
Just your lips, and Lowell would lean in
To listen, his ear right next to your mouth,
Then look up smiling and roll over to tell me
What you said, that since you'd passed over
You'd heard why women live longer than men—
Because they wear big diamond rings.

II.

She is sitting three pews ahead of me
At the Methodist church on Wilshire Boulevard.
I can make out one maple leaf earring
Through the upswept fog bank of her hair
—Suddenly snapped back, to stay awake.
A minister is lamenting the forgetfulness
Of the laws, and warms to his fable
About the wild oryx, "which the Egyptians
Say stands full against the Dog Star
When it rises, looks wistfully upon it,
And testifies after a sort by sneezing,
A kind of worship but a miserable knowledge."
He is wearing, now I look, the other earring,
Which catches a bluish light from the window

Behind him, palm trees bent in stained glass
Over a manger scene. The Joseph sports
A three-piece suit, fedora in hand.
Mary, in a leather jacket, is kneeling.
The gnarled lead joinder soldered behind
Gives her a bun, protruding from which
Two shafts of a halo look like chopsticks.
Intent on her task, her mouth full of pins,
She seems to be taking them out, one by one,
To fasten or fit with stars the night sky
Over the child's crib, which itself resembles
A Studebaker my parents owned after the war,
The model called an Oryx, which once took
The three of us on the flight into California.
I remember, leaving town one Sunday morning,
We passed a dwarfish, gray-haired woman
Sitting cross-legged on an iron porch chair
In red slacks and a white sleeveless blouse,
A cigarette in her hand but in a silver holder,
Watching us leave, angel or executioner,
Not caring which, pursuing her own thoughts.

III.

Dawn through a slider to the redwood deck.
Two mugs on the rail with a trace
Still of last night's vodka and bitters.
The windchimes' echo of whatever
Can't be seen. The bottlebrush
Has given up its hundred ghosts,
Each blossom a pinhead firmament,
Galaxies held in place by bristles
That sweep up the pollinated light

In their path along the season.
A scrub jay's Big Bang, the swarming
Dharma of gnats, nothing disturbs
The fixed orders but a reluctant question:
Is the world half empty or half full?
Through the leaves, traffic patterns
Bring the interstate to a light
Whose gears a semi seems to shift
With three knife-blade thrusts, angry
To overtake what moves on ahead.
This tree's broken under the day.
The red drips from stem to stem.
That wasn't the question. It was,
Why did we forget to talk about love?
We had all the time in the world.

What we forgot, I heard a voice
Behind me say, was everything else.
Love will leave us alone if we let it.
Besides, the world has no time for us,
The tree no questions of the flower,
One more day no help for all this night.

LATE NIGHT ODE

It's over, love. Look at me pushing fifty now,
   Hair like grave-grass growing in both ears,
The piles and boggy prostate, the crooked penis,
   The sour taste of each day's first lie,

And that recurrent dream of years ago pulling
   A swaying bead-chain of moonlight,
Of slipping between the cool sheets of dark
   Along a body like my own, but blameless.

What good's my cut-glass conversation now,
   Now I'm so effortlessly vulgar and sad?
You get from life what you can shake from it?
   For me, it's g and t's all day and CNN.

Try the blond boychick lawyer, entry level
   At eighty grand, who pouts about the overtime,
Keeps Evian and a beeper in his locker at the gym,
   And hash in tinfoil under the office fern.

There's your hound from heaven, with buccaneer
   Curls and perfumed war-paint on his nipples.
His answering machine always has room for one more
   Slurred, embarrassed call from you-know-who.

Some nights I've laughed so hard the tears
   Won't stop. Look at me now. Why *now*?
I long ago gave up pretending to believe
   Anyone's memory will give as good as it gets.

So why these stubborn tears? And why do I dream
    Almost every night of holding you again,
Or at least of diving after you, my long-gone,
    Through the bruised unbalanced waves?

Horace iv.i

from HAZMAT

2002

FADO

Suppose my heart had broken
Out of its cage of bone,
Its heaving grille of rumors—
 My metronome,

My honeycomb and crypt
Of jealousies long since
Preyed on, played out,
 My spoiled prince.

Suppose then I could hold it
Out toward you, could feel
Its growling hound of blood
 Brought to heel,

Its scarred skin grown taut
With anticipating your touch,
The tentative caress
 Or sudden clutch.

Suppose you could watch it burn,
A jagged crown of flames
Above the empty rooms
 Where counterclaims

Of air and anger feed
The fire's quickening flush
And into whose remorse
 Excuses rush.

Would you then stretch your hand
To take my scalding gift?
And would you kiss the blackened
    Hypocrite?

It's yours, it's yours—this gift,
This grievance embedded in each,
Where time will never matter
    And words can't reach.

GLANUM

at the ruins of a provincial Roman town

So this is the city of love.
I lean on a rail above
Its ruined streets and square
Still wondering how to care
For a studiously unbuilt site
Now walled and roofed with light.
A glider's wing overhead
Eclipses the Nike treads
On a path once freshly swept
Where trader and merchant kept
A guarded company.
As far as the eye can see
The pampered gods had blessed
The temples, the gates, the harvest,
The baths and sacred spring,
Sistrum, beacon, bowstring.
Each man remembered his visit
To the capital's exquisite
Libraries or whores.
The women gossiped more
About the one-legged crow
Found in a portico
Of the forum, an omen
That sluggish priests again
Insisted required prayer.
A son's corpse elsewhere
Was wrapped in a linen shroud.
A distant thundercloud
Mimicked a slumping pine
That tendrils of grape entwined.

Someone kicked a dog.
The orator's catalogue
Prompted worried nods
Over issues soon forgot.
A cock turned on a spit.
A slave felt homesick.
The underclass of scribes
Was saved from envy by pride.
The always invisible legion
Fought what it would become.

•

We call it ordinary
Life—banal, wary,
Able to withdraw
From chaos or the law,
Intent on the body's tides
And the mysteries disguised
At the bedside or the hearth,
Where all things come apart.
There must have been a point—
While stone to stone was joined,
All expectation and sweat,
The cautious haste of the outset—
When the city being built,
In its chalky thrust and tilt,
Resembled just for a day
What's now a labeled display,
These relics of the past,
A history recast
As remarkable rubble,
Broken column, muddled
Inscription back when

Only half up, half done.
Now only the ruins are left,
A wall some bricks suggest,
A doorway into nothing,
Last year's scaffolding.
By design the eye is drawn
To something undergone.
A single carving remains
The plunder never claimed,
And no memories of guilt
Can wear upon or thrill
This scarred relief of a man
And woman whom love will strand,
Their faces worn away,
Their heartache underplayed,
Just turning as if to find
Something to put behind
Them, an emptiness
Of uncarved rock, an excess
Of sharp corrosive doubt.

•

Now everything's left out
To rain and wind and star,
Nature's repertoire
Of indifference or gloom.
This French blue afternoon,
For instance, how easily
The light falls on debris,
How calmly the valley awaits
Whatever tonight frustrates,
How quickly the small creatures
Scurry from the sunlight's slur,

How closely it all comes to seem
Like details on the table between
Us at dinner yesterday,
Our slab of sandstone laid
With emblems for a meal.
Knife and fork. A deal.
Thistle-prick. Hollow bone.
The olive's flesh and stone.

JIHAD

A contrail's white scimitar unsheathes
Above the tufts of anti-aircraft fire.
Before the mullah's drill on righteousness,
Practice rocks are hurled at chicken-wire

Dummies of tanks with silhouetted infidels
Defending the nothing both sides fight over
In God's name, a last idolatry
Of boundaries. The sirens sound: take cover.

He has forced the night and day, the sun and moon,
Into your service. By His leave, the stars
Will shine to light the path that He has set

You to walk upon. His mercy will let
You slay who would blaspheme or from afar
Defile His lands. Glory is yours, oh soon.

•

Of the heart. Of the tongue. Of the sword. The holy war
Is waged against the self at first, to raze
The ziggurat of sin we climb upon
To view ourselves, and next against that glaze

The enemies of faith will use to disguise
Their words. Only then, and at the caliph's nod,
Are believers called to drown in blood the people
Of an earlier book. There is no god but God.

He knows the day of death and sees how men
Will hide. Who breaks His covenant is cursed.
Who slights His revelations will live in fire.

He has cast aside the schemer and the liar
Who mistake their emptiness of heart for a thirst
That, to slake, the streams of justice descend.

.

Ski-masked on videotape, the skinny martyr
Reads his manifesto. He's stilted, nervous.
An hour later, he's dropped at the market town,
Pays his fare, and climbs aboard the bus.

Strapped to his chest is the death of thirty-four
—Plus his own—"civilians" on their way
To buy or sell what goods they claim are theirs,
Unlike our fates, which are not ours to say.

Under the shade of swords lies paradise.
Whom you love are saved with you, their souls
In His hand. And who would want to return to life

Except to be killed again? Who can thrive
On the poverty of this world, its husks and holes?
His wisdom watches for each sacrifice.

ORCHID

Now that you are gone, you are everywhere.
        Take this orchid, for instance,
its swollen lip, the scrawny stalk's one
        descended testicle
as wrinkled as rhetoric on the bar-scene stump,
        the golden years since
jingling in its purse. How else signal the bee?

In my swan-clip now languish urgent appeals
        from the usual charities
lined up to be ignored. But your flags are up:
        I see the flapping petals,
the whorl of sepals, their grinning come-on.
        Always game, again
I'd head straight for the column's sweet trap.

Ducking under the puckered anther cap
        to glide toward the stiff,
waxy sense of things, where male and female
        hardly matter to one's heady
urge to pull back the glistening lobes
        and penetrate the heart,
I fell for it every time, the sticky bead

laid down on my back as I huddled there
        with whatever—mimicking
enemy or friend, the molecular musk
        of each a triggering lure—
wanted the most of me. Can I leave now too?
        I have death's dust-seed
on me. I have it from touching you.

CANCER

And then a long senescent cell—though why,
Who knows?—will suddenly refuse to stay
In line, the bucket brigade of proteins meant
To slow or stimulate the tissue's growth
Will stumble, so the cells proliferate
And tumors form while, deep within,
Suppressor genes, mutated, overlook
The widening fault, the manic drive to choke
On itself that fairy tales allot the gnome
Who vainly hammers the broken sword in his cave,
Where malignant cells are shed into the blood
Or lymph, cascading through the body's streams,
Attaching themselves to places where we breathe
And love and think of what cannot be true.

2.

It is as if, the stench intensified
And strong or weak alike now swept away,
The plague in Athens hurried its descent
By fear, a symptom leaving the stricken loath
To fight for life who had defied the great
Spartan ranks themselves, the sight of skin
Inflamed, the thirst, the dripping anus took
Hold of them until, in tears, they broke.
The dead in piles around them, a hecatomb
To gods who, like those mongrel dogs who crave
A corpse they drag to safety through the mud

To feast upon, had disappeared, their dreams,
According to Thucydides, seethed
With images of forsaken, drowning crews.

3.

She had lost the bet, and in her sunken eyes
The birthday she had over and over prayed
To die before was offered like a present.
(Dressed in a party hat, I sat with both
My parents by the bed.) A toast was made.
Through the pleated, angled straw she took in
A burning mouthful of champagne, and rebuked
Her son-in-law for his expensive joke,
Drawing, hairless, an imaginary comb
Through memories of what pleasure anger gave,
Then smiled, "I'd stop all this if only I could."
Even at ten I sensed that she had seen,
Staring at me, what would be bequeathed.
My mother slowly closed her eyes. We knew.

PENIS

Years of sneaking sidelong glances toward the one
    At the next urinal's gaping mouth—
Between classes, between buses, between acts,
    In dorm or disco, rest stop or Ritz—
Assemble them now in a sort of line-up:
    Bald, one-eyed, red-faced, shifty suspects,
Each generic, all so individual—
    Hooded, lumpish, ropy, upcurving,
Anchovy or shark, the three-inch alley cat
    Or blood-choked panther whose last droplet,
Back-lit by porcelain, is wagged free to fly
    In a bright sterile arc, its reversed
Meniscus shattered by the soon swirling flush.
    But that slice-of-life in the Men's Room
In retrospect seems an idle pantomime,
    Old desires or anxieties
Projected onto a stranger's handful
    Of gristle, the shadowy dumb show
Our schoolroom puppets once swooped and wiggled through
    Back when any sense of difference
Posed as curiosity's artless cut-outs.
    Only years later was I haunted
By a premonition of something I thought
    I didn't have, or have enough of
—Poor Punch, fingered, limp, flung back into his case.

.

Who knows what early memories are redeemed,
    What primitive rites re-enacted,
By our masculine version of mother-love?
    What daily unconscious tenderness

Is lavished here, such fastidious grooming
    Rituals for the wrinkled baby
Capuchin. Each man's member every morning
    May be gingerly held and jiggled
Inside his Jockey shorts or lazily scratched
    Through silk pajamas—in any case,
Fondled, its crimpled, sweat-sticky, fetid skin
    Lifted off the scrotal water-bed
And hand-dried as if in a tumbler of air.
    Later, tucked behind the clerk's apron
Or the financier's pinstripes or the rapper's
    Baggy jeans, our meek little Clark Kent
Daydreams at his desk of last night's heroics,
    Hounded by a double life blackmailed
By grainy color shots of summer-cabin
    Or backseat exploits that had won praise
From their pliant, cooing co-conspirators.
    But now, absently readjusted,
As if fresh from cold surf, his ideal is just
    The bud of classic statuary.
The marble is hard, the soulful cub withdrawn.

•

So, the old questions linger on unanswered.
    Why in the fables on Greek kraters
Do those of the ephebes always stick straight out?
    Why is it the last part of a man's
Body to age? Though function may no longer
    Follow form, its chthonic shaft and crown
Retain maturity's rugged majesty.
    What Ovid might once have figured out
As a shepherd who'd struck a king in disguise,
    Or Plato have thought in an aside

The haphazard tail of white in the pot where
    His abstract egg was hard-boiling into halves
Soon in search of some way to resume the shell
    Of an identical privacy,
Scientists today measure as Anyman's
    Lowest common denominator,
A demonic's tutorial in the means
    Of his being manipulated
By unpredictable powers far beyond
    His knowing but not his sad sensing.
Do I wish my own rose at will, and stayed put,
    And was just, say, two inches longer?
Sure. So who doesn't think he's inherited
    An apartment too small for his plans?
Do I cancel the party, or gamely shrug?

•

"But why," Jane asks, "is something silly at best
    And objectively ugly at worst
The focus of so much infatuation?"
    Cults thrive on cloying contradictions.
Shrewd and aloof, women are thought to enjoy
    What it does, the petulant master
They devour, or the wheedling spongy slave
    They finally love to rub the wrong way.
And men? Men! Men are known to appreciate
    What it stands for. History books have this
In common with off-the-rack pulp romances.
    Small men with big ones, big men with small,
Lead lives of quiet compensation, power
    Surging up from or meekly mizzling
Down to the trouser snake in their paradise.
    If love's the religion with the god

That fails, is it because blood goes to his head?
    No, it's that after the night's tom-toms
And fire-dances are over and he's sulking
    In his shrine, sadness beats him hollow.
Asked by nagging reporters once too often
    Why, despite the count of body bags,
We were in Vietnam, LBJ unzipped
    His fly and slapped it on the table.
"Gentlemen, this is why," he barked. "This is why."

TATTOOS

1.

Chicago, 1969

Three boots from Great Lakes stumble arm-in-arm
        Past the hookers
     And winos on South State
To a tat shack. Pissed on mai tais, what harm
      Could come from the bright slate
Of flashes on the scratcher's corridor
Wall, or the swagger of esprit de corps?

Tom, the freckled Hoosier farmboy, speaks up
        And shyly points
     To a four-inch eagle
High over the Stars and Stripes at sunup.
      A stormy upheaval
Inside—a seething felt first in the groin—
Then shoves its stubby subconscious gunpoint

Into the back of his mind. The eagle's beak
       Grips a banner
     Waiting for someone's name.
Tom mumbles that he'd like the space to read
     FELIX, for his small-framed
Latino bunkmate with the quick temper.
Felix hears his name and starts to stammer—

He's standing there beside Tom—then all three
       Nervously laugh
     Out loud, and the stencil

Is taped to Tom's chest. The needle's low-key
     Buzzing fusses until,
Oozing rills of blood like a polygraph's
Lines, there's a scene that for years won't come off.

Across the room, facedown on his own cot,
      Stripped to the waist,
   Felix wants Jesus Christ
Crucified on his shoulder blade, but not
     The heartbroken, thorn-spliced
Redeemer of punk East Harlem jailbait.
He wants light streaming from the wounds, a face

Staring right back at those who've betrayed him,
      Confident, strong,
   With a dark blue crewcut.
Twelve shading needles work around the rim
     Of a halo, bloodshot
But lustrous, whose pain is meant to prolong
His sudden resolve to fix what's been wrong.

(Six months later, a swab in Vietnam,
      He won't have time
   To notice what's been inked
At night onto the sky's open hand—palms
     Crawling with Cong. He blinks.
Bullets slam into him. He tries to climb
A wooden cross that roses now entwine.)

And last, the bookish, acned college grad
      From Tucson, Steve,
   Who's downed an extra pint
Of cut-price rye and, misquoting Conrad
     On the fate of the mind,

Asks loudly for the whole nine yards, a "sleeve,"
An arm's-length pattern of motives that weave

And eddy around shoals of muscle or bone.
                    Back home he'd signed
              On for a Navy hitch
Because he'd never seen what he's since grown
              To need, an *ocean* which . . .
But by now he's passed out, and left its design
To the old man, whose eyes narrow, then shine.

By dawn, he's done. By dawn, the others too
                    Have paid and gone.
              Propped on a tabletop,
Steve's grappling with a hangover's thumbscrew.
              The bandages feel hot.
The old man's asleep in a chair. Steve yawns
And makes his way back, shielded by clip-ons.

In a week he'll unwrap himself. His wrist,
                    A scalloped reef,
              Could flick an undertow
Up through the tangled swash of glaucous cyst
              And tendon kelp below
A vaccination scallop's anchored seaweed,
The swelling billow his bicep could heave

For twin dolphins to ride toward his shoulder's
                    Coppery cliffs
              Until the waves, all flecked
With a glistening spume, climb the collar-
              Bone and break on his neck.
When he raises his arm, the tide's adrift
With his dreams, all his watery what-ifs,

And ebbs back down under the sheet, the past,
    The uniform.
    His skin now seems colder.
The surface of the world, he thinks, is glass,
    And the body's older,
Beckoning life shines up at us transformed
At times, moonlit, colorfast, waterborne.

2.

Figuring out the body starts with the skin,
    Its boundary, its edgy go-between,
The scarred, outspoken witness at its trials,
    The monitor of its memories,
Pleasure's flushed archivist and death's pale herald.
    But skin is general-issue, a blank
Identity card until it's been filled in
    Or covered up, in some way disguised
To set us apart from the beasts, whose aspects
    Are given, not chosen, and the gods
Whose repertoire of change—from shower of gold
    To carpenter's son—is limited.
We need above all to distinguish ourselves
    From one another, and ornament
Is particularity, elevating
    By the latest bit of finery,
Pain, wardrobe, extravagance, or privation
    Each above the common human herd.
The panniered skirt, dicky, ruff, and powdered wig,
    Beauty mole, Mohawk, or nipple ring,
The pencilled eyebrow above Fortuny pleats,
    The homeless addict's stolen parka,
Facelift, mukluk, ponytail, fez, dirndl, ascot,

The starlet's lucite stiletto heels,
The billboard model with his briefs at half-mast,
    The geisha's obi, the gigolo's
Espadrilles, the war widow's décolletage . . .
    Any arrangement elaborates
A desire to mask that part of the world
    One's body is. Nostalgia no more
Than anarchy laces up the secondhand
    Myths we dress our well-fingered goods in.
Better still perhaps to change the body's shape
    With rings to elongate the neck, shoes
To bind the feet, lead plates wrapped to budding breasts,
    The sadhu's penis-weights and plasters,
The oiled, pumped-up torsos at Muscle Beach,
    Or corsets cinched so tightly the ribs
Protrude like a smug, rutting pouter pigeon's.
    They serve to remind us we are not
Our own bodies but anagrams of their flesh,
    And pain not a feeling but a thought.

But best of all, so say fellow travellers
    In the fetish clan, is the tattoo,
Because not merely molded or worn awhile
    But exuded from the body's sense
Of itself, the story of its conjuring
    A means defiantly to round on
Death's insufferably endless emptiness.
    If cavemen smeared their bones with ochre,
The color of blood and first symbol of life,
    Then peoples ever since—Egyptian
Priestesses, Mayan chieftains, woady Druids,
    Scythian nomads and Hebrew slaves,
Praetorian guards and kabuki actors,
    Hells Angels, pilgrims, monks, and convicts—

Have marked themselves or been forcibly branded
  To signify that they are members
Of a group apart, usually above
  But often below the rest of us.
The instruments come effortlessly to hand:
  Fish bone, razor blade, bamboo sliver,
Thorn, glass, shell shard, nail, or electric needle.
  The canvas is pierced, the lines are drawn,
The colors suffuse a pattern of desire.
  The Eskimos pull a charcoaled string
Beneath the skin, and seadogs used to cover
  The art with gunpowder and set fire
To it. The explosion drove the colors in.
  Teddy boys might use matchtip sulphur
Or caked shoe polish mashed with spit. In Thailand
  The indigo was once a gecko.
In mall parlors here, India ink and tabs
  Of pigment cut with grain alcohol
Patch together tribal grids, vows, fantasies,
  Frescoes, planetary signs, pinups,
Rock idols, bar codes, all the insignia
  Of the brave face and the lonely heart.

The reasons are both remote and parallel.
  The primitive impulse was to join,
The modern to detach oneself from, the world.
  The hunter's shadowy camouflage,
The pubescent girl's fertility token,
  The warrior's lurid coat of mail,
The believer's entrée to the afterlife—
  The spiritual practicality
Of our ancestors remains a source of pride.
  Yielding to sentimentality,
Later initiates seek to dramatize

Their jingoism, their Juliets
Or Romeos. They want to fix a moment,
   Some port of call, a hot one-night-stand,
A rush of mother-love or Satan worship.
   Superstition prompts the open eye
On the sailor's lid, the fish on his ankle.
   The biker makes a leather jacket
Of his soft beer belly and nail-bitten hands.
   The call girl's strategic butterfly
Or calla lily attracts and focuses
   Her client's interest and credit card.
But whether encoded or flaunted, there's death
   At the bottom of every tattoo.
The mark of Cain, the stigma to protect him
   From the enemy he'd created,
Must have been a skull. Once incorporated,
   Its spell is broken, its mortal grip
Loosened or laughed at or fearlessly faced down.
   A Donald Duck with drooping forelock
And swastikas for eyes, the sci-fi dragon,
   The amazon's ogress, the mazy
Yin-yang dragnets, the spiders on barbed-wire webs,
   The talismanic fangs and jesters,
Ankhs and salamanders, scorpions and dice,
   All are meant to soothe the savage breast
Or back beneath whose dyed flesh there beats something
   That will stop. Better never to be
Naked again than not disguise what time will
   Press like a flower in its notebook,
Will score and splotch, rot, erode, and finish off.
   Ugly heads are raised against our end.
If others are unnerved, why not death itself?
   If unique, then why not immortal?
Protected by totem animals that perch

Or coil in strategic locations—
A lizard just behind the ear, a tiger's
    Fangs seeming to rip open the chest,
An eagle spreading its wings across the back—
    The body at once both draws death down
And threatens its dominion. The pain endured
    To thwart the greater pain is nothing
Next to the notion of nothingness.
    Is that what I see in the mirror?
The vacancy of everything behind me,
    The eye that now takes so little in,
The unmarked skin, the soul without privileges . . .
    Everything's exposed to no purpose.
The tears leave no trace of their grief on my face.
    My gifts are never packaged, never
Teasingly postponed by the need to undo
    The puzzled perfections of surface.
All over I am open to whatever
    You may make of me, and death soon will,
Its unmarked grave the shape of things to come,
    The page there was no time to write on.

3.

New Zealand, 1890

Because he was the chieftain's eldest son
            And so himself
        Destined one day to rule,
The great meetinghouse was garishly strung
        With smoked heads and armfuls
Of flax, the kiwi cloak, the lithograph
Of Queen Victoria, seated and stiff,

Oil lamps, the greenstone clubs and treasure box
           Carved with demons
        In polished attitudes
That held the tribal feathers and ear drops.
           Kettles of fern root, stewed
Dog, mulberry, crayfish, and yam were hung
To wait over the fire's spluttering tongues.

The boy was led in. It was the last day
           Of his ordeal.
        The tenderest sections—
Under his eyes, inside his ears—remained
           To be cut, the maze run
To its dizzying ends, a waterwheel
Lapping his flesh the better to reveal

Its false-face of unchanging hostility.
           A feeding tube
        Was put between his lips.
His arms and legs were held down forcibly.
           Resin and lichen, mixed
With pigeon fat and burnt to soot, was scooped
Into mussel shells. The women withdrew.

By then the boy had slowly turned his head,
           Whether to watch
        Them leave or keep his eye
On the stooped, grayhaired cutter who was led
           In amidst the men's cries
Of ceremonial anger at each
Of the night's cloudless hours on its path

Through the boy's life. The cutter knelt beside
           The boy and stroked

The new scars, the smooth skin.
From his set of whalebone chisels he tied
    The shortest one with thin
Leather thongs to a wooden handle soaked
In rancid oil. Only his trembling throat

Betrayed the boy. The cutter smiled and took
        A small mallet,
    Laid the chisel along
The cheekbone, and tapped so a sharpness struck
    The skin like a bygone
Memory of other pain, other threats.
Someone dabbed at the blood. Someone else led

A growling chant about their ancestors.
        Beside the eye's
    Spongy marshland a frond
Sprouted, a jagged gash to which occurs
    A symmetrical form,
While another chisel pecks in the dye,
A blue the deep furrow intensifies.

The boy's eyes are fluttering now, rolling
        Back in his head.
    The cutter stops only
To loop the blade into a spiralling,
    Astringent filigree
Whose swollen tracery, it seems, has led
The boy beyond the living and the dead.

He can feel the nine Nothings drift past him
        In the dark: Night,
    The Great Night, the Choking
Night, the All-Brightening Night and the Dim,

The Long Night, the Floating
Night, the Empty Night, and with the first light
A surging called the War Canoe of Night—

Which carries Sky Father and Earth Mother,
        Their six sons borne
    Inside the airless black
The two make, clasped only to each other.
        Turning onto his back,
The eldest son struggles with all his force,
Shoulder to sky, straining until it's torn

Violently away from the bleeding earth.
        He sets four beams,
    Named for the winds, to keep
His parents apart. They're weeping, the curve
        Of loneliness complete
Between them now. The old father's tears gleam
Like stars, then fall as aimlessly as dreams

To earth, which waits for them all to return.
        Hers is the care
    Of the dead, and his tears
Seep into her folds like a dye that burns.
        One last huge drop appears
Hanging over the boy's head. Wincing, scared,
He's put his hand up into the cold air.

THE AGAVE

The villa's switchback garden path,
between the potted railing and the sea
and under the canopy of overlapping pines,
winds through what can grow under them:
plants from a moon orbiting Venus maybe,
brambly fig, yucca, holm oak, firethorn,
and silvery, bloated succulents—
The Penitent, Dead-Child's-Fingers,
Mother's-Stool, Chapel-of-Solitude.

The agave beside the stone bench,
where I have sat heavily all day,
reaches out in all directions,
its meaty, grizzled leaves each
the length of a man, each edged
with back-turned venomous thorns,
thumbnail billhooks in ranks down
from the empurpled spike at its tip.
The largest leaf, right next to me,
has so bent under itself, the spike
has come around and gone up through
another part of itself—the heart, say,
or whatever comes to as much as that.
Yesterday the gardener told me
it could take thirty years for the spike
slowly—never meaning to, thinking
it was headed toward the water-glare
it mistook for the little light that kept
not coming from above—slowly

to pierce its own flesh, to sink its sorrow
deep within and through its own life.

It only took me a month.

THE FEVER

The fever has lasted three days.
Layers of skins and weavings
were first heaped on the bed
but nothing kept out the cold
that shook my body
like a crackhead mother
angry because her baby
won't stop crying.
Then another body crawled in
beside me, held me—
she throws the blue baby
down the furnace chute,
the ceiling hisses at
the ice pack's beaded apathy,
the hidden air, the voices,
the voices all too calm.
I'm hauled up, they listen
to my back. What can it say?
They listen to my front.
A deep breath. Does this hurt?
So much I can't answer.
They ease me back down.
The one beside me slips away.
I can hear him in the next room.
He's laughing. He's given up.

This is how love feels, they write.
So which one am I in love with?

THE INFECTION

In those days I used to refuse the medicine
because the infection then made it hurt so
when I came, hurt so that the pain—
its intolerable scalding contractions,
the knot choked by appetite, desperate
to advance and retreat, to thrash further
inside its own swollen sentence,
the little useless gash, the bitter spasm—
each night left me frightened and smiling.
The tears had rinsed my eyes, the whining
stilled any desire to repeat myself.
I thought of it as a kind of mutilation,
less of my body than of my longing not to have one.
Afterwards, I would limp to the bathroom
for a hot washcloth and hold it to myself,
and then to my face. The cloth smelled
of the rotten hyacinths, their stalks snapped,
their milky petals gone brown and sticky,
I would pass each weekend, thrown to the back
of the stalls, pots of them, at the flower market.
I went to the window, put the cloth on the stone
ledge. Until it dried, it would be my standard,
my scorn and seamark, my flag of surrender.

LATE AFTERNOON, ROME

Down the street, on the path to the oratory,
the stations of the cross—huge bronze slabs,
their ordinary agonies modernized to poses
on a fashion runway—have been wired shut.
A river of swallows sheers off course again
around air-locked spurs of warmth or chill.
The sun is out late, panning for gold
in the silt of our ochre upper floors.
Everything is looking up for a change.
Isn't that white capsule on the blue tablecloth
the daily jumbo jet? It's so far beyond
the cross and thorns, beyond the drawstring
of birds, beyond the last light down here.
And there's already a glass of water on the table,
for the pill I was meant to take hours ago.

THE BOOKCASE

My empty bookcase yawns and rises
from its paint job, white asphalt
newly laid over a grid of back streets,
the chill of what assurance supports it all
still in the air, no music, no voices.
Who wants to live with what he knows?
While I sit on the storage boxes,
my double's slowly making his way
among shop windows and bloody altars,
holding pages to the light, changing
sex to distance himself from force
or faithfulness, the household demons.
It's late. Opportunities are multiplying.
I am what I did? I am what I wait for?
I feel something returning, like a book
put back on the shelf, slid between
names like mine, my story, my fault.

HOTEL BAR

The saxophonist winds up "My Romance,"
the song with a scar. In the red lacquer ceiling,
the night's raw throat, I can just make out
lampshades the color of a smoker's breath.
One is at our table. Across sits a woman
in tiny furs from before the war, the mouth
of one gnawing on the tail of the other,
like comets. A sudden brightness onstage,
a flaring spot, flashes on the nodding brass.
The little thud at a nova's heart predicts
the gradual, dimming ebb and flow
of light—or love—soon enough burnt out,
remembered only as desire's afterglow.
So which one has the room key? Neither of us
wants to guess what won't ever be opened.
Something is found in a galactic pocket.
Something is left behind on a chair.
The elevator doors close soundlessly.
A constellation of numbers rises in order.
Again, the argument from design's invoked.
Tomorrow we'll get to go back over it all,
what's partially false and almost always true,
as in "My romance doesn't need a thing but you."

A TOUR OF THE VOLCANO

After colliding with a cloudberg, the chopper
sinks through more, like feelings gone soft
around the edges, forming shapeless moist
masses and as easily dissolving, until underhead
we approach the ashen, lopsided cones,
the brimstone stench of steam, the mess of gods.
Headphones dip into the sliding plates
dragged over soft forces divided by stress,
some fracturing crust of indifference
through which the buried magma seeps.
Or have I got it all wrong again?
Does he mean instead that, once home,
after we're back, set down, driven off,
the sunset's backwash sloshing
in the rearview's little sac of sorrows,
the tremors will start again, the leakage?

LITTLE ELEGY

But now that I am used to pain,
Its knuckles in my mouth the same
Today as yesterday, the cause
As clear-obscure as who's to blame,

A fascination with the flaws
Sets in—the plundered heart, the pause
Between those earnest, oversold
Liberties that took like laws.

What should have been I never told,
Afraid of outbursts you'd withhold.
Why are desires something to share?
I'm shivering, though it isn't cold.

Beneath your window, I stand and stare.
The planets turn. The trees are bare.
I'll toss a pebble at the pane,
But softly, knowing you are not there.

OUIJA

Years ago—long enough at least for bitter
Leaves to have cooled at the bottom of a cup
Then brimful and steaming with insecurities—
Four spellbound friends were huddled around
What might as well have been a campfire,
Their shadows thrown back on the world
By candlelight, the flames of anticipation
Fed by skittish questions of whatever voice
Any one of them had felt clearing its throat
Inside the jelly lid with its toothpick pointer
Patrolling a border of hand-drawn letters—

Not theirs, of course, the timidly curious
Weekend houseguests in rainy Stonington,
But JM's, the loom from which bolts of blues
Lay stacked on his desk, *Ephraim*'s final galleys.
The master had been unexpectedly
Summoned by redundancy—a family crisis—
But insisted . . . look, the steak's been marinating,
There's plenty to drink, the weather forecast's glum.
They'd stay? And why not take an idle turn
At the board? His Honda was barely in reverse
When Mickey's mop and pail were blithely tossed

Aside and motley, ill-fitting robes assumed—
In their case, a cheap imitation mantle
That, like any religion, risked mocking
What it worshipped. But then, how else learn
What can't be taught than play the earnest fool?
Left alone with a luster and delirium
About to be cut with callow, flavorless slush,
They pulled their chairs up to the round table,

Guarded by votive griffins, a saltcellar,
And a spineless cactus that waited patiently
Under a bite-size crystal hanging from the dome.

Roach clip. Jug wine. The conventional aids
To inspiration were reluctantly foresworn
In favor of seltzer and cold credulity.
They sat there edgily, hour after hour,
Watching the voices muster into words—
As when, between the scenes of a play, the stage
Is briefly darkened but still slightly visible,
Enough for us to see the stagehands moving
Furniture around, the props of what's to come—
So that what had clumsily been transcribed
Into a notebook later came clear in ways

Each might have made light of there in the dark.
A——, for instance, at thirty buffed and tan
But oddly pious and almost too eager for word
Of how immanent the Beyond would turn out to be,
A lens in the black box of lives led here below.
He begins by chance with Agul, a priest of Aton,
Standoffish and abstract. *Egyptians not concerned*
With sin, only singularity. We wait for sunrise.
Friends exchange light. Love, light, are one.
I breathe your light. Aton knows your aspect.
And for those who don't care, whose beliefs start

When their eyes are shut? *Night is sun for others.*
Doggedly the acolyte buttonholes the board.
At last one Mary Wentworth gently picks up
The extension, a London mother and mystic
Two centuries dead. *Your soul, sweet A——,*
The shape of a healthy body, shelters under my wing.

Wing? *Down is warmer than up.* Up?
The Pharisees are cold on their mountain tops.
They will not sin & so they freeze. Your body
Sins to warm your heart. How easily tenderness
Rinses the dirty hands temptation lathers.

Then B——, saddled with a Fifties adolescence
Spent peeping at encyclopedia cross-sections
And nudist colony glossies—all shrivel and sag—
Until transfixed by martyred Oscar's wit,
Its gay science devoted to curing the heart,
Shyly asks, after combing his hair, for Himself.
The Other Life, within us or abroad,
Acts—and why not?—as if it had all the time
In either world, exaggerating its courtesies.
Wilde extends an invisible gloved hand
To B——, who stutters about his nervousness.

Confession is good for one's soul & one's royalties.
I sold my lower depths & made a good thing of them.
But his own feelings . . . for the young man, say?
Bosie was ornamental. That was enough.
No real love then? Your wife? *Constance*
Was as her name suggests. That was not enough.
Though Paris is, of course, better on the whole,
I think most of Oxford, where, donning robes,
Pater drew on airy nothing to burn with a flame
Of the first water, in whose heat our damp clay
Was fired into well-wrought urnings. ("The ease,"

B—— marvels, "with which a practiced stagecraft
Flicks its iridescent fan!") *No window*
Can without some dressing up long hold
A discerning eye. For birds of our feather

The pen that is a plume adds panache.
But—oh, this is as it must be written—
A thousand admiring eyes in the world
Of letters finally matter less than the one
Understanding heart in a country retreat.
Blushing, B—— withdraws, interested only
In how prudently to spend his overdraft.

Then C——, whose reedy, wire-rimmed pretense,
Goosed by Southern manners and a French degree,
The saccharine-coated pill B—— had been swallowing
For a decade, insinuates his clubman's smarm
And succeeds in raising static on the line.
A giggling Indian scout—*ice filled my seeing,*
Great ice-haired mounts, English—trails off
To a corpuscle who or which insists eternity
Is *the plucked tension between limit and nothing.*
A yawn gets passed around. A Chinese sage
Wanders across the screen, dropping fragments

Of a fortune cookie. *We do not gain the moon*
By telling her to be still. Fingers in silhouette
Mug redwood trees, or German armaments
Tycoon, or chef, or silent movie vamp,
The manic Cuisinart finally shredding
Soul into a slaw of nonsense syllables.
The others glower at C—— and call a break,
When suddenly, as from another room,
A stricken whisper: *Was I that humpback*
At whom you laughed when you believed me
Out of hearing? Oh sweet betrayal, my bridegroom!

And D——. (But why "D——"? His name was Drew.
I knew him, loved him.) A tenant of his body,

He was hurt by everything he took for remedy—
Waiting tables, acupuncture, coke—
And longed to leap against the painted drop,
Some grand pirouette center stage, sweat whipped
Into the spotlight, sequined corsair or satyr.
He asks for Isadora. *Hail, friend!*
Why do they never book me anymore?
Drew then nudges into the dressing room
With a question. Will I ever dance like you?

You know in your bones. I died broken on the wheel
Of circumstance. Now it's just tableau vivant.
The happiness of the body is all on earth.
The beauty of the body in motion and repose
I wanted to give, long after it was probable.
Drew's charged resolve saw him through the drill
(Temp job to tryout) of making a name for himself,
Until he met the dancer who infected him.
The virus flic-flacked through his system, aswirl
In cells that faltered and too soon abandoned
The soloist whose stumble a falling curtain concealed.

For that matter, you too, JM, have gone
And done it, become a voice, letters on a page—
Not like love's sweet thoughtless routine
But a new romance, hazard and implication,
Promises as yet unmade, possibilities
Slipping, say, from N to O . . . —Oh,
Why will words cohere and dissolve on this blank
And not their darker meanings, an unspoken grief
I've reached for and felt sliding as if over
Poster board smoothed by years of being used
To giving back the bright presence drawn

Up from within yourself, your starry heart
So empty, so large, too filled with others
Not to fear an unworthiness indwelling.
You took everything on faith but death,
An old friend's or the breathless lining
Of any new encounter, so that fresh acolytes,
Once back home, would remark with wonder
On your otherworldliness. What they failed
To see was something that has just now begun
To sink in on me: how little your detachment
Had to do with the demands of a formal art

Or a mind at once too sovereign and too spent
By being trolled for schools of thought or feeling.
Stage fright can apply or smear what make-up
Seems necessary for any evening's encores,
And lines rehearsed before the smoked mirror's
Critical gaze can turn to ashes in the mouth
When spoken to some poor stick mugging there
Who you hope will stay the night and fear
May last until the end. How seldom, I sense,
You gave yourself up, how often instead
Had to borrow back what had already been lent.

Even the board is under wraps in a closet upstairs.
Funny, I've not tried to do it since you died,
Even for a simple jabbing toward the consoling *Yes*
In answer to the obvious questions posed
By missing you. Or have I instead been fearing
The *No*—the not-happy *No,* the not-there *No?*
Or had you perhaps been receding all along—
Like those friends of a quarter century ago,
Faded to vanishing points like death or California,

Where everything to be lost is finally regained,
The figures of speech for once beyond compare?

No. I *can* hear your voice from the other side,
That kingdom-come memory makes of the past,
The old recordings, the stiffening onionskin
Letters your Olivetti punched out from Athens
Or Isfahan, notebook cities shaped
By anecdotes of love—no, antidotes,
Spelled out to be kept suspended at a distance,
As now I imagine your nights with pencil and cup.
From my seat, somehow above or below the table,
Your hand moving steadily back and forth
Across the board seems like a wave goodbye.

in memory of James Merrill

from MERCURY DRESSING

2009

MERCURY DRESSING

To steal a glance and, anxious, see
Him slipping into transparency—
The feathered helmet already in place,
Its shadow fallen across his face
(His hooded sex its counterpart)—
Unsteadies the routines of the heart.
If I reach out and touch his wing,
What harm, what help might he then bring?

But suddenly he disappears,
As so much else has down the years . . .
Until I feel him deep inside
The emptiness, preoccupied.
His nerve electrifies the air.
His message is his being there.

ER

I hesitate to mention now the time
I hesitated—was it weeks or months?—
Before telling him I was leaving, leaving for good,
So that, in the end, it was he who left me,
And my fear of his decision, or no . . . well,
His tonelessly announcing it one night,
Only that, always that, has clouded the scene,
Not unlike the way the years of happiness
Until that day, all of them a delusion,
Had prevented my recalling just how long
I'd waited to discover my feelings at the start.
Two weeks—no, less—on my own, secret cell
Phone calls, a rented post office box,
The desperate joking, the passionate or-elses,
Seemed only to discover the nowhere
I lingered in, the time I wanted to postpone
Hurting myself or him, the time I wanted
To wait until I could turn into something
He would never leave. Years later, forcing me
To divide the shoebox full of snapshots
Or the letters from our long-dead companions,
He waited while I chose, through tears, the things
I didn't want to see, and did not look back
Through the closing door, though it only seemed
As if he were standing there and I was falling
Back, back to a time when I couldn't delay
Any longer, the time I leaned down to select
My lot, lying there on the ground, in the field,
Where I recognized so many others waiting their turn.

•

In Plato's *Republic,* there is an explanation of this.
Twelve days after his death in battle, the body of Er—
Son of Armenius, a hero of legend in far Pamphylia—
As torches were readied, came to life again on his funeral pyre,
And told what he had seen of the other world,
That his soul in a crush of companions had journeyed
To a mysterious place, two openings, it seemed, in the earth
And two others above, between them the seats of judges
Who bound men to their sentences, that they should climb
Or descend, the symbols of their deeds fastened to their backs.
But Er was told only to watch and bear the message back to men.
He saw the dead arrive, dusty with travel, and the souls
Of those already saved step down into a meadow to meet them.
Those who knew one another embraced and wept at tales
Of what they had endured and seen, while those above
Told of delights to come, of injustices reversed, of tyrants
Cast into terrors worse than they had themselves inflicted.
Er then looked up at a column of light to which the chains
Of heaven were attached that held the spindle of Necessity,
Its eight hollowed whorls broadening into spangled ranks
Of wheeling planetary orbits moving as they must,
Each sounding a note in harmony with the rest, and the Fates
Adding their overtones, their hands touching, turning,
Guiding the spindle through its past, its present, its future.
As Er looked on, each mortal soul was asked to choose its genius.
The first were told not to be careless, the last not to despair—
Each would have the lot of his desire, the length of a new life.
Er stood in astonishment as, one after another, men and women,
Because the memory of their previous lives was still so strong,
Asked to be animals in the next, no matter bird or beast,
A blameless, unknowing being not in love with death.
The soul that had once been Orpheus chose the life of a swan,
Not wanting to be born of a woman, hating
The race of women who had murdered him.

Others chose sparrow or horse or, remembering their pain,
An eagle that could circle the slain in their bloody armor,
Slowly circle, high over what men do to themselves.
Then each was given a cup of Unmindfulness
From which some carelessly drank too much
And some too little, so that the past would haunt them.
Er himself was kept from drinking, and how
His body was returned he could never say,
But as the others were driven, like stars shooting,
Up to their births in the world, torches were lit
And Er suddenly woke and found himself
Lying on a pyre, his old parents in tears.

·

In the end, because I took too long to decide,
The bird-lives on the ground there to choose from
Meant I would have to live far from home.
I chose the farthest, the common tufted warbler,
Native to the Maghreb, a small bird,
The size of a fist, the color of wet sand,
My tail brushed with berrystain, my crest
Opening to the sides its fan of mandarin
Barbules gemmed with black incipient beads,
My call a calling, *er-rand, er-rand, er-rand.*
I can fly to find direction out and sing
Only to attract the echoing air,
But my task, an hour before dawn, is to help
Summon the halfhearted day from its sleep
As the dark begins to tip reluctantly.
My limping chirr, its admonition falling
Into place, glides through the oasis citrus grove,
Switches of scrub beginning to stir and stretch,
To remind who hears it there is work to be done,

Word to be sent ahead of happiness,
Of noon on an iridescent scarab wing,
Of the dank leaf mold and warted rind,
Of the peace in our hours now, for all but them,
Those humans who shout and slash and smell of flesh.
One of them stands alone, every morning, looking
Into water, silently moving his lips. I stay
To keep watch, and something comes back, a sense
From some other life, that because he has never been hurt,
He is impossible to love. For now, he is my errand.

for Edmund White

SELF-PORTRAIT AS AMUNDSEN

When as a boy I lay with no clothes, no cover,
The window open to winter, I would watch for the sun
To appear, as today its sharp edge has finally
Sliced through the months of waiting with companions
I loathe because I cannot do this alone.
So the adventure, too long dreamt of and precisely
Planned, will start tomorrow, the calculation
To be mounted against chance. My eye is on the timepiece
Of days, on how we measure the setting out
Of depots to support our coming back to tell
The story to the king whom we allowed to send us.
The sledges are loaded, the dogs—half of them
To be killed to feed the other half—impatient.
Come "night" we will stop, and by "day" move forward
Across the waste of pack ice without a horizon
Before us. No living thing can be replaced.
On a cloud, a compass error, a tangled bootlace
The action may depend, the last secret lost.
The metallic light, the fear of rival black specks
Miles off but hour by hour coming closer,
These are thought by others unscalable barriers.
I have always known that I would be the one
Not just who found but wanted to find the abstract,
Meaningless point on which the planet turns.

THE FRAME

Fussily ornate and merely decorative,
Wreaths of fruited branchlets and fluttering ribbons
    Echoing the scrolled plasterwork
    On moldings around the mirrored
        Parlors where a patron
        Could straighten his collar,
    Reliefs embellished with glass beads
    To mimic his beloved's brooch,
Rosettes cast in pairs and affixed with foil and wax,
Then coated with gesso and gilded to seem carved,

Or cross-hatched textures scratched onto the surfaces
Of curling leaves and hammered for the fine matting
    Of metal with tiny pocked points,
    The crinkled foil of gold pressed down
        Onto the moistened bole
        For a burnished veneer
    That aligns the soft candlelight
    On the apostle's face with what
Shines more severely from the Savior's fingertip,
Is not the sort of frame I prefer to enclose

What I should figure on as an allegory
Of someone's sense of what he puts between himself
    And the world. I prefer the frame
    Whose entablature seems to shield
        What it displays, withhold
        What has been given it
    To help explain the mysteries
    Of the child sent to redeem us.
From architrave to plinth, balusters upholding
What the crested lunette oversees, the rigid

Vocabulary of antiquity admits
No distractions, nothing to lead the eye away
    From the perfected cityscape
    And room, where a sad pale woman
        Under a stone cherub
        The color of the clouds
    Holds something that she knows will die.
    A friend sits beside her, peeling
An apple. In the distance, three men on horseback
Look up at her window, the darkness in a frame.

RESIGNATION

I like trees because they seem more resigned
to the way they have to live than other things do.

—WILLA CATHER

Here the oak and silver-breasted birches
Stand in their sweet familiarity
While underground, as in a black mirror,
They have concealed their tangled grievances,
Identical to the branching calm above
But there ensnared, each with the others' hold
On what gives life to which is brutal enough.
Still, in the air, none tries to keep company
Or change its fortune. They seem to lean
On the light, unconcerned with what the world
Makes of their decencies, and will not show
A jealous purchase on their length of days.
To never having been loved as they wanted
Or deserved, to anyone's sudden infatuation
Gouged into their sides, to all they are forced
To shelter and to hide, they have resigned themselves.

SORROW IN 1944

1.

The name in the register was *Pinkerton, Frank,*
The plate on his Ford parked next to Cabin Eight
The dented oil-and-orange of the Golden State.
The Pinewoods Motor Court, on the riverbank
A mile south of the Heart Mountain camp,
Seemed more welcoming each visit—not a home
But a familiar port of call where, cold and alone,
He can walk the wards of desire with a signal lamp.

His father's Navy ties had kept him free—
No bedding, kettle, and hot plate on E-Day.
Milton Eisenhower's signature
Was clearance enough, but only for him, not her.
The years in Wyoming, she said, have been "okay."
He stared at her mittens, love's own internee.

2.

They'd met at a blood drive, winter of '42,
Her father a clerk, her mother a picture bride.
Pearl Harbor meant they were on the same side.
His father was dead, his mother said she knew
"About the things my husband had done abroad,
About the suicide . . . mistakes of the past . . .
A love that made no sense and could not last.
Under his uniform, what man isn't flawed?"

He filled out a form. She glanced at it and then
Looked up. She saw a future, he the face
Among the fallen blossoms. They agreed to meet.
It was already hard to cross a street
Without an angry stare, or find a place
To share a pot of tea, again and again.

3.

Her name is Tanabata, after the queen
Who wove the Milky Way's gauzy grisaille,
Her loom but three weak stars in the eastern sky.
Her herdsman-lover can cross the Celestial Stream
On the seventh day of the seventh month, a span
Of birds his passageway, and, as he nears,
The sallow river-mist begins to clear,
The floodtide loses ground where once it ran.

She has waited there for him on the other shore,
A year at a time. She has waited through her tears,
Through all the promises made and broken before.
But there he is! The familiar shape appears.

      At the water's edge,
      Her robe of rushes and cranes
      Slowly getting wet,

      She can hardly remember
      In which lifetime they had met.

4.

The weeks in the assembly center's horse stalls—
The stench, the straw, the lack of privacy—
Had made the boxcar and the barracks seem
A privilege. Actual beds and tarpaper walls,
Canned Vienna sausages and kumquats,
The Rockies beyond a barbed-wire fence.
The guards were tight-lipped and indifferent,
Like their old neighbors, who waved and forgot.

The world beyond the camp was a weekly newsreel.
She pretended not to mind the soot and the noise,
Or notice the boys who sat near her at meals—
Those swoony, moon-bit pepper-shaker boys.
She sewed, and gave a day at the clothing bank,
Chewed her pencil, and sometimes wrote to Frank.

5.

Only once had he ever heard her name.
Sitting in the chair of his hospital room
Toward the end, his father suddenly assumed
He knew the story but never whom to blame.
"So long ago. . . . What was I thinking of?
They said she called you Sorrow. I don't know why.
We give the silliest names to the things we love.
I killed her, I guess. I called her Butterfly."

After the funeral, his mother told him more.
She hated what she couldn't understand.
He watched her twist her handkerchief and cry.
She told him of the blindfold, the knife on the floor . . .
Already items in memory's contraband.
The sun sank quickly. *He called her Butterfly.*

6.

He has driven twice a month, for two years now,
Through endless miles of broccoli and sugar beets,
Then east across the mountains to a road that meets
Another, despite the map, and leads somehow
To the Pinewoods' nondescript, unfastened door.
Only the slant-eyes down the way have a past.
A "salesman" is what he's called himself if asked,
But no one seems to care much anymore.

Each night at nine he's at the prison gate.
A pack of Chesterfields, and a familiar face
Is furtively waved in. He's allowed an hour.
He and Tanny sit and complicate
Their lives, while rival gangs of schoolboys chase
A barking mongrel toward the security tower.

7.

Just sitting there, at the table for BLOOD TYPE B,
She seemed to Frank at first too young, all wrong,
The sweater and saddle shoes, the hair too long.
But the longer he spoke to her, the more he could see
That time and chance had converged on this one girl.
His duty now was clear. What might it mean—
All the years between them merely a screen
He could slide to reveal the cherry trees aswirl—

To love her who long ago had this same face?
He waited until he was sure she'd seen through
His social calls more than she'd admit.
He hesitated, then in an awkward embrace
Vowed to be constant and compassionate.
(Oh, how not tell the truth and still be true?)

8.

She and her parents sent away for good . . .
The world at war . . . the papers filled with hate . . .
She was twenty, he was forty-eight . . .
Everything conspired as it could
To keep them apart. Even the words they spoke
Fell short of what they felt. Sometimes silence
Seemed more to them than mere convenience.
Tanny would fidget or hum. Frank would smoke.

Her father asked him to smuggle letters or take
A message to the general, but he refused,
Not from fear but apathy, or heartbreak.
He wanted only what she might suddenly choose,
Though for herself she asked nothing, like love
Or like stars, those wounds in the tender flesh above.

9.

Each night—on those nights he visited the camp—
He'd turn the corner by Block Thirteen and stop,
Expecting to find a badly painted backdrop,
A pale body on a bloodsoaked, floodlit ramp,
And the tearful applause that echoed in his dreams.
Instead, she was sitting there on the mess hall steps
And shyly smiled. Again, his promise was kept.
Again, she helped him past the years between.

She let him hold her hand while she described
A basketball game. He looked down at the ground
And smiled to hear just how the girls would shriek,
How they ran across the muddy court and found
An opening in the air. She'd nearly died!
By then he wasn't listening, but he let her speak.

10.

When all the wells in the holy city had failed
And only Matsumura's, as if fed by a spring,
Remained, he allowed the afflicted people to bring
Their buckets, until one day—or so the tale
Unfolds a servant drowned and the old priest
Went to the well, where he saw in the water there
The image of a woman combing her hair,
A ghost from his past or a spirit unreleased.

A week later, during a violent storm,
The woman visited his room and revealed
She was a dragon's mirror in a woman's form.
No harm would come so long as he kept her concealed.

    The well, drained and raked,
    Yielded a blazoned hairpin
    And a mirror rim.

    When he searched its emptiness
    He saw what had haunted him.

LINGERING DOUBTS

1.

The honeybees dance and are understood,
But their point is always and only nectar.
Achilles spoke with the gods, and all
They wanted was his spear through Hector.

2.

By the Senate's decree, in the heart of Rome
No ominous soldiers were allowed
Except in hollow triumphs where,
More than the general, plated and proud,
The whispering slave amused the crowd.

3.

From pre-hab to re-tox in under a year,
The cynic had run his terror to ground.
The man in the mirror was merely glass.
The world was just "Another round."

4.

The woman giving birth
Was standing near a bed,
The child apparently worth
The risk that lay ahead.
"Don't be stubborn. Here,
Lie down," he crossly said.
She winced and shook her head.
"Spoken just like a man.
Lie down? A bed? That's where
The trouble first began."

5.

The day he left, he said I knew the reason.
Look at the trees. Love only lasts a season.
For years since then, I've stared at them and seen
Only their blackened branches beneath the green.

THREE OVERTURES

I. Consecration of the House

How many did I live in before I had my own?
During the war, my father in the Pacific,
There was my widowed grandmother's
With its collection of French clocks
And closet doors, mostly the must
Of a turn-of-the-century wardrobe.
Next, the newly demobbed's semidetached
And its neighborhood's first television set,
A cherrywood box on legs with its ten-inch
World Series that played to a crowd
White-knuckling old-fashioneds.
Finally, the tile-roofed white stucco
Suburban, memory's first homestead
Because living there—my own room at last!—
Coincided with a fogbound sexual dawning
That rose, flushed, in a corner of its attic
But had less to do with my body than the books
Stolen from Wanamaker's that touched
On Reproduction, accompanied by
Photographs of one toad atop another.
I would hold my own tiny reptile
And imagine a milky pudding of incipient
Tadpoles until a translucent drop
Of something surfaced with less pleasure
Than, in the basement, a sheet on a clothesline
Came up on Act I in which, having collected
Tickets and delivered the Prologue, who starred
As the Frog Prince, accompanied by his sisters
As cellophaned water beetles, insisted

He eat from the plate and sleep in the bed
Of a person the stage director had cleverly
Represented as an invisible royal presence,
Haughty, deceitful, probably an early role
Model not perfected until a decade later
At the college grill's monthly Gay Night . . .
But that was two intermissions further along.
Back in the preteen's cellar theater—so like
The attic's erotics in which, as in dreams,
One is always the protagonist—I couldn't have
Guessed the greasepaint had also smeared on
A coarseness and meanness I perpetuated
Out of timidity, a fear of reproducing myself
Except as someone else, someone noble
If warted, unafraid because unaware
I had already started out on the wrong foot
By supposing I was safe with a secret life,
Something so ordinary as wanting to please,
Wanting to hide in the sources of pleasure.

II. *Calm Sea and Prosperous Voyage*

At an age when the extra baggage is the paraphernalia
Of parents, both of whom—if only I'd had to—
Would already have been packed and labeled
NOT WANTED ON VOYAGE, I was almost on my own,
Fifteen, aboard the *Queen Mary,* feeling
The mattress in my stateroom's upper berth
For lumps and staring out the porthole
Opposite at the alluring distant shores
Of New Jersey. Tugs were backing us out
Of everything familiar. It was time to shave.
While my bunkmates—this was a chaperoned

Grand Tour for what the brochure had termed
"Precocious" adolescents—were crowding
The promenade deck to watch Lady Liberty wave
Goodbye, I was at the tiny sink's mirror,
Staring at my own precociousness,
The delicate but distinct shadow of fuzz
Above my lip and the half-dozen stray
Hairs, a few here, a few there, but enough
To convince me the first bold step
To adulthood was to lather it all up
For the safety razor I had purchased
From a druggist who'd squinted and shrugged.
I was alone. I was ready. I had seen the ads
And the actors, had often sat on the tub's edge
To study my father's assured technique.
I knew the stuttering downward stroke,
The rising slow-motion flick of the wrist.
I had laid out a version of my newly sophisticated
Self on someone else's bed: my dark suit,
My wash-and-wear shirt and regimental tie.
There were still two hours before the Captain's
Bon Voyage Dinner. I had long since scanned
The passenger list and devised a flexible
Introduction with just enough flattery and French
In it to impress anyone standing nearby
Who overheard half of it. Time to shave.
From the hissing aerosol can shot a gob
Of foam I petted my face with, the double-sided
Blade was clamped into place, and I cocked
My head for a better look at a ragged
Sideburn where, clearing my throat, I tentatively began.
What little there was yielded without a struggle,
When suddenly there was a screw loose,
Or the bow thruster backfired or the rudder reeled—

Something jammed and the ship seized up
With intermittent convulsions I decided
Unwisely to ignore until several red alerts
On cheek and chin demanded that I stop.
My debut as an adult later that evening
Included the ignominy of five scraps of tissue
Plastered by the blood they staunched
Onto the curiosity of tablemates who looked
Beyond me in order to see right into my vapidity.
Perhaps I *had* grown up, then. Even a single hair
Casts a shadow. Sitting there in public,
A failure at the simple tasks, my vanity on display,
I might have already realized we use the first part
Of our lives to render the rest of it miserable.

III. Light Cavalry

The charge of the light cascade
From the disco globe's orbiting
Spray of incandescent pricks
Had electrified me long enough.
I'd invested a decade in the hunt-
And-peck system of trying
Not to find myself—though *that*
Was a maze of abrupt right angles
And false leads even my shrink
Failed to decipher—but someone else,
Someone just to stay home with.
Night after night at the Nibelheim,
Through a scrim of exhaled Kools,
I'd made out the same old tricks
Lined up at the bar, as if having taken
Their positions at curtain time—

The repairman nursing his Bud,
The receptionist hugging his stool,
The goggle-eyed poli-sci postgrad,
The dishy interns in scrubs,
Bankers, biologists, bricklayers
(Even, oops, Stephen Spender once),
Each with his bit part to play,
His wary banter or boogie.
I rarely scored for lack
Of trying, wearied by the whole
Lump-in-the-throat approach
And pain-in-the-ass retreat.
So, resolute, hunched over a map
Of my future, I made a decision.
I would lie low for a month,
Hoping the tide would wash up
Flopping new prospects worth more
Than the loneliness of forced companionship.
Time was up. The time was ripe.
I chose a Saturday night to storm
The bar and steal away with a man
For good—the someone, an anybody,
A man I could admit wanting
To "love," if that's the word for giving
Your "heart" away, for doubting
What until that day you'd most believed.
My strategy was to sit next
To the first customer I saw wearing a tie,
A necktie, all knot and design,
Standing in, it seemed, for a set
Of assumptions and hesitations
I shared, or wanted to share.
I entered and scouted and spotted
The only one who matched my profile,

Then simply, rudely, slid into the booth
Where he was sitting with three or four
Now startled and resentful friends,
Introduced myself and started talking
Without noticing more than his four-in-hand.
(The next morning, the rest came clear:
Short, curly-haired, sharp-featured,
With fingers propped on his chin
Both delicate and slowly drumming.)
He was, it turned out, a pianist
And willing to accompany my off-key
Renditions of the usual storm and stress.
As we left the bar together that night,
And lived happily ever after for a year,
I knew the second step in the right direction
Would be the hardest, but didn't care.
I had the life I wanted, didn't I? Didn't I?

TREES, WALKING

And he took the blind man by the hand, and led him out
of the town; and when he had spit on his eyes, and
put his hands upon him, he asked him if he saw aught.

And he looked up, and said, I see men as trees, walking.

After that he put his hands again upon his eyes, and made him
look up: and he was restored, and saw every man clearly.
      —MARK 8:23–25

If the sun were a hot bright blue, the daylight
    Would shine on a planet cold-blooded
To the spectrum of what now we can make out
    Of shapes in the distance—the sun itself, say,
Or the blighted ash over there near the, the . . .
    Whatever it might be. To be told
About the colors and textures we could not
    Actually see, or to listen
For how the petal tip begins to turn brown
    And the paint on the kitchen cabinets
Is sallower than it was when the baby
    Was in diapers, would be to loosen
The string of molecular ties that binds us
    To one another. As if in parallel
Lines down the center of a ballroom waiting
    For the gavotte to begin, we gaze
Across at our partners and take our bearings
    By what will momentarily spin
Out of our vision, the settee and lampstand,
    The string quartet poised for the downbeat,
The women in black standing with lemonade
    Along the wall. We need a second

To know and be known by what we see around
    Us, and what we see through the window,
The men smoking cigars on the balcony,
    And billowing up far behind them
The stand of horse chestnuts on the horizon.
    We know where we are, what we are meant
To do next by what we can keep an eye on,
    The world's child now its worried parent.
I can still spot my father, two decades dead,
    In my doctor's thick medical file
And in his warning when he looks up from it,
    My inheritance a condition
I could live without. The past blurs my future.
    The blood sugar choking my system
So that I can see my right foot but not feel
    The internist's pinprick on its toes
Has also clouded my sight and anything
    Three feet away takes on the thickset
Haziness that some second-generation
    Impressionist would spoil a nude with.
TV's talking heads on mute all look the same,
    Bobbing owlets on the barn's rafter.
Taking in the news hour with a martini,
    I watch each day's car bomb explosion
Through the bleared perspective history provides,
    The sense that people will keep fighting
Over the same wooden idol or acre
    Of nowhere because once as children
They had been grabbed and told to look their fathers
    Right in the eye. Now the machine guns
Are bigger than the boys who aim them at each

Other, whole brigades of them, marching
Toward the sun that, while we weren't looking, turned red.

•

Three cypresses advancing toward me have paused
      By the bulging edge of the river
With its stench of corpses. I can smell it too
      On my fingers. When the trees lean down
To lap the water, they leave the western sky
      Starless, a deformed hole in the night
Where the hunter ought to prowl or the altar
      Stand for its vigil. I can hear dogs,
Both menacing and scared, barking at the trees.
      Behind me, the palms are throwing bones
In a game of chance. I have been told they are
      Palms, and I have known palms by their pine-
Cone trunks and stiff-leafed fronds. They are all speaking
      Of how their dreams, when they follow them,
Have saved their lives, and of how any people
      Who invent just one god are lazy.
They wave their fans but the heat leaves them listless,
      Unable to move. They have fallen
Silent. Then, closer to me now, the words start.

•

When wise men say that others know too little
      Of themselves, think of King Cambyses.
He would slap the serving boy and pound his fist
      On the table, shouting for the wine
From that province in the south, the one for guests,
      The one he'd asked for in the first place.
A candle fell and set fire to a woven

Basket near the queen's ladies, who rose
In fear and retired, their hands across their mouths.
   Enraged, the king demanded they stop
And return to their seats, how dare they presume
   To leave before he has said they may.
He called for the dancers but would not watch them.
   He called next for his secretary
But had nothing to say for his wax tablet.
   The look in his eyes was faraway.
His counselor Praexaspes had seen that look
   Too often before, not of desire
But of vacancy, and if a king was not
   Himself the kingdom was in danger.
His eyes searching the room for disloyalty,
   Praexaspes approached—as if to bring
His master word of a small scandal—
   The king's couch from behind and leaned down
To whisper if he might offer some advice
   To His Majesty. The king grunted.
He who drinks with moderation is prepared
   To command and protect his people,
He said, for the king's ear alone, then quickly
   Coughed into his fist and backed away.
Cambyses turned and looked him full in the face,
   Then smiled. We shall see, he roared, and called
For more wine, and as he gulped it down, he stared
   At Praexaspes, daring him to look
At anything but the lavish gilded shells,
   One after another, his slaves brought,
Each brimming with the syrupy wine that spilled
   Onto his robe. You think I have lost
Control of myself, he had wanted to say,
   But the words came out confusedly.
The king laughed at himself, then ordered the son

Of Praexaspes to stand facing him,
In the middle of the room, his left arm raised
   High above his head so he would look
Like a once delicate acacia lightning
   Had struck a limb from and left to grow
Crookedly. The young man at first tried to smile
   At the king and the ladies, but then
Hesitated and glanced toward his old father,
   Who slowly nodded. The son complied.
Cambyses reached out shakily for his bow
   And without ever turning his head
Told his friend he would not only shoot his son
   But shoot him to the very middle
Of his heart. On that last word the arrow streaked,
   The body slumped to the marble floor.
Praexaspes stood there wide-eyed, ashen, silent.
   The king growled at a guard to go cut
Open the dead youth's chest and bring him the heart.
   It was brought to the king, who held it
Out for the father to see. The arrowhead
   Had gone precisely halfway into
The center of the bloody thing in his hand.

   •

And what I first heard sounded like an arrow
   Flashing past me. *Farther,* it had hissed.
But when it happened again, I heard *Father.*
   I backed right up to a tree and felt
A feathery branch on my head, in my hair,
   Back and forth, circling over my head.
Again, behind, soft as a breeze now, *Father.*
   But at the same time the cypresses
By the river grew huge and dark and started

To come closer. A thunderous wind
Made them shudder, parts of them even broke off
    And fell near me, jagged, smeared with mud.
I forgot about the other trees running
    Across the hill and the tree behind
Suddenly seemed to take hold of me and shook
    Me so that I was thrown to the ground
And lay trembling in a bank of leaves and soot.
    It was time I was falling out of.
The trees came from nothing and then disappeared.

•

At the second intermission of *Manon*
    We were bored and on a third vodka
When Teddy set his glass on the bar and said
    That he needed to confide in me.
"If I turn a blind eye on the betrayal
    I am admitting two faults of mine.
I am a fool to trust the love of my life,
    And I am willing to let his cruelty
Continue if that means I can overlook
    My own fears of inadequacy—
I'm too old by a decade, too dull in bed,
    Too complacent about faded charms.
If I tell him that, instead of men, I see,
    Say, *trees* walking out of his bedroom
When I return unexpectedly at dawn
    From a business trip, who would I be
Kidding, hmm? The lover I can't live without?
    Or, jeez, the man I have to live with?"
The lobby chimes meant we had ten minutes left.
    "That last time, the whole apartment . . . well . . .
The peonies on the coffee table stank,

The fridge was full of yogurt gone off,
The light over the bathroom sink had blown out.
    All this in a weekend? A lifetime?
What the hell had I gotten wrong the whole time?
    If he's never loved me, why can't he
Have the decency not to spit in my face? . . .
    Oh, but why am I telling *you* this?
The truth is, nothing in one's life is deserved.
    Maybe deceit is some form of grace.
Or maybe love is just the ability
    To overlook what is bound to hurt."
So. Embarrassed by his pain, I let the talk
    Drift back to the night's performances . . .
To the French . . . to *anything* but his story,
    As we took our seats for the third act.
The director's conceit had set the Gambling Scene
    In a forest whose trees had baize trunks
And rustling gold coins for leaves, though long before
    The charges of cheating flew, my head
Was on my chest. Lukewarm applause around me
    At the curtain scuttled half the dream,
But later, in the cab, some of it came back.
    Teddy, twice his age, glossily lit
From underneath as if in a tabloid shot,
    Was squatting over a cellar hole.
There was a man in the shadows behind him
    Wanting to help. His arms were held out.
Everything on this earth has a natural
    Enemy able to destroy it,
He explained, and told Teddy to dress in black
    Leather encrusted with small mirrors,
Then to go down into the hole with a net
    And capture the hissing basilisk.
Once his eyes had adjusted to the darkness,

He could make out in a far corner
The creature he had been sent to bring to light.
   The cock's head, the scaly curved body—
None of the fable was true. It was a tree
   Aflame with a scalding light. He stared
Until there were tears in his eyes and nothing
   Else, just tears that ran like a river
Down his face, on whose bank was another tree,
   Branches weeping into the water,
The black shape of the man who stood behind him.

•

I never understood why I had to leave
   The city. I could find my way there
As around the rooms of my own house, its walls
   What held my hand, its stalls and doorways
The spaces between other people, its noise
   A pathway through the darkness silence
Was for me. Perhaps he needed me near trees,
   Near things as large as my memories
Of them. It was a tree that once betrayed me.
   When I was a child and my father
Had taught me his tools and shown me their uses,
   I one day by accident injured
My cousin's mule. His father had been drinking
   And came demanding that he be paid.
Before my father could discover the truth,
   The man had spotted me and shouted.
I ran and climbed into a neighbor's thorn tree
   But he came and shook its trunk. I fell.
He grabbed me. The sunlight blazed off his knife blade.
   The slash, a jagged X, crossed through
My face. The cloth they used to soak up the blood

Has been, as it were, over my eyes
Ever since. The tree I thought would protect me
    Gave me to the dead of night instead.
My father did all of my weeping for me.
    It was not hard to see what I felt,
But when they said of a man that he had been
    Unfaithful, or will be *immortal,*
It was as if I could understand the word
    Face but not entirely realize
It meant *eyes* and *mouth* somehow put together.
    I was thought stupid and kept apart.
Our cares are cowards and never come alone.
    My father died, I was sent away,
My body did not work the way it should have.
    It was my cousin who first heard of
The healer and then told me, dressed me, brought me
    To a man who never asked questions
Except with the fingers of his hand, my scars
    The story he seemed to tell himself.
A hot dry air was blowing. Trees around us
    Wheezed and scolded the dust on their leaves.
Someone had spit on me. I was used to that.
    I felt its contempt dry on my cheek.
The wind grew stronger, too loud to understand
    Anything but the healer's demand
To open my eyes and tell him what I saw.
    I saw my cousin's father coming
Toward the tree, his face angry, his mouth open
    But no words in it. Then the tree moved.
All the trees moved, walking away from the man
    And his knife. He shouted after me.
I thought I heard him tell me to look again.
    The tree stopped and I climbed down from it
Into the stranger's arms, looking at his eyes,

His mouth. I reached and put my finger
Into it. He stared as I put my finger
    Then into my own mouth. Everything
Around me was so bright I was forced to close
    My eyes. If I ever open them
Again, all I hope to see is my father.

GOING BACK TO BED

Up early, trying to muffle
the sounds of small tasks,
grinding, pouring, riffling
through yesterday's attacks

or market slump, then changing
my mind—what matter the rush
to the waiting room or the ring
of some later dubious excuse?—

having decided to return to bed
and finding you curled in the sheet,
a dream fluttering your eyelids,
still unfallen, still asleep,

I thought of the old pilgrim
when, among the fixed stars
in paradise, he sees Adam
suddenly, the first man, there

in a flame that hides his body,
and when it moves to speak,
what is inside seems not free,
not happy, but huge and weak,

like an animal in a sack.
Who had captured him?
What did he want to say?
I lay down beside you again,

not knowing if I'd stay,
not knowing where I'd been.

FULL CAUSE OF WEEPING

Love, sending much blood toward the heart, causes many vapors
to issue from the eyes, and the coldness of sadness, retarding the
agitation of these vapors, causes them to change to tears.

—RENÉ DESCARTES

The actor taught to recall his dying pet
Can trick an audience that wants to believe she's alive
Into swallowing the tears he sheds onstage,
Cordelia's body in his arms a golden retriever
Once laid to rest in an Idaho backyard.
Or take the mourner who makes her living by wailing
At wakes, hired by kin to help reclaim
From death's silence the one who lies there unmoved.
Each is prompted by an insincerity
I've accused myself of, who weep at Loews
But at the loss of friends am barely upset.

Whenever Mammy climbs the stairs with Melanie,
Heartgrief in her face, explaining that Bonnie
Cannot be locked up inside a casket
Because she has always been afraid of the dark,
My throat tightens, the hot tears surge,
My sleeve hides half the scene, then the whole,
Yet with a pitiably precise flashlight
I can make my way through memories of my father,
Striding toward his open grave pit
Dry-eyed, wondering what I'm expected to say,
Impatient with the strangers who stand there numbly.

For those who collect their tears, later to drink
Like a thick wine, or place on the Last Day's scales,
The impulse to seduce is all the body's.

But I prefer revenge to magic, like the wife
Whose husband was enslaved to help construct
The Great Wall, and when she searches for him
Only to find that he has died and been thrown
Into the ground under the Wall, she bursts
Into a flood of tears that, in time, washes away
A hundred miles of the Wall and its overlords.
When the mind wells up, the heart too can think.

But what do I know? I enjoy a happy ending
Because of its illusion, the scrim through which
The death of love can all too clearly be seen.
Sadness is a stimulant I crave like any other.
Secretions and secrets, letting things out
Or keeping them in, are my threatened jewel box,
The tribute I pay myself for tearing down
The trellis on which a spindly grief is trained.
How sweet the bitterness has become in my mouth,
A rancid honey that, drop by drop, drips
From the certainty of being nothing.

Heavenly hysteria, or the way music makes
Our melancholies, distances us from despair,
And emptying time of its eternities
Dries the eye, but which of us would yield
His voluptuous clinging to things that pass?
Without suffering, life would be unbearable.
The heart's open wound, where lovers play,
And ice packs on the next morning's swollen
Second thoughts, wrung of their consolations,
Seem in themselves somehow to create
The strange thirst our two teardrops slake.

In mine is the bridal suite at the Paradise
And, tiled with chips of noon, its infinity pool,
The size of a compact car, where on the edge
Of the world's overspill the slim young groom,
Nightcap in hand, is lazily humping his bride
From behind, her groans exaggerated to please
His vanity, while he stares out at the stars,
The ones that fall and the ones that stay there
In their stories, sword and prey, lust and grief.
Slowly, they circle around the point of it all.
He holds up his glass, rattling the ice.

In yours, I can see the frigid bottom water
Oozing along the ocean floor, the warmer
Current above it, without coagulating
Salt and darker duties, running free
In sun or spindrift, without the pressure
Slowly to move toward what will ruin it.
The dead and the living float together in layers,
This thin sheet of fresh water atop
The denser open sea of souls. Listening
From the surface I can hear the low unhappy
Pulse of love, and what will echo after.

A VIEW OF THE SEA

The argument had smoldered for a week,
Long enough for the fine points of fire,
Banked from the start against self-righteousness,
To have blurred in the pale ash of recrimination.
I couldn't tell which wound would be the deeper—
To stay on, behind the slammed door,
Forcing you to listen to me talk about it
With others, or to leave you altogether.
What caused the argument—another crumpled
Piece of paper with a phone number on it—
Felt at last as lost as all the bright
Beginnings, years back. And then . . .
                                        And then
You were standing at the sink with your back to me
And must have sensed me there behind you, watching.
Suddenly you turned around and I saw in your eyes
What all along had been the reason I loved you
And had come to this moment when I would be forced
To choose but could not because of what I had seen,
As when the master of the tea ceremony,
Determined to embody his ideal,
Had constructed a room of such simplicity
That only a decade of deliberating its angles
And details was in the end required of him,
A wooden floor so delicately joined
That birds still seemed to sing in its branches,
Three salmon-dyed silken cushions
On which the painted quince petals trembled,
A pilled iron kettle disguised as a sea urchin,
Each cup the echo of cloud on wave,
And on the long low wall, a swirling mural
Of warlords and misty philosophers,

The Ten Most Famous Men in the World,
Floating at its center the gold-leafed emperor . . .
Who, rumors having reached the court,
Was invited to come approve the great design,
But when he saw himself as merely one
Of ten, declared that because the master's
Insult was exceeded only by his skill
He would be allowed to take his own life
And have a month to plan the suicide.
The master bowed, the emperor withdrew.
At the month's end, two aged monks
Received the same letter from their old friend,
The master, who had now built his final teahouse—
An improvisation, a thing of boards and cloth
On the mountain in the province of their childhood—
Inviting them for one last cup together.
The monks too wanted nothing more,
The sadness of losing their friend to his ancestors
Eased by the ordinariness of his request.
But they were feeble and could not make the climb.
Again the master wrote, begging them
To visit—he was determined to die the very day
They came and in their company, and besides,
He reminded them, from the mountain they would have
A view of the sea, its round immensity
The soul's own, they could never elsewhere command.
The two monks paused. Their duty to a friend
Was one thing, but to have at last a view of the sea,
A wish since each had been a boy bent
Over pictures of its moonswept midnight blue. . . .
So they agreed and undertook the difficult journey,
Sheer rock, sharp sun, shallow breaths until
They reached the top. The master was waiting for them,
The idea of leaving life already in his looks,

A resignation half solemn, half smiling.
He led them past a sapling plum he noted
Would lean in the wind a hundred years hence.
A small ridge still blocked the sea, but the master
Reassured them it would be theirs, a memory
To return with like no other, and soon, soon.
They came to his simple house, a single room,
But surrounded by stunted pines and thick hedges
They could not see beyond. Patience was urged.
Inside, they were welcomed with the usual silences,
With traditional bows and ritual embraces.
At the far end of the room, the two cups of water
On the floor, the master explained, were for them
To purify their mouths with before the tea was served.
They were next told to lie on their bellies and inch
Toward the cups, ensuring a proper humiliation.
The monks protested—they had come to see their friend
Through to the end, to see his soul released,
Poured like water into water—and where, after all,
Was the unmatched view he had promised them?
They would, he countered, all have what they wished
If they yielded as they must to this ceremony.
The master waited. The monks slowly, painfully
Got to their knees, then to the straw mat,
Their arms outspread as they had been instructed,
And like limbless beggars made their way across
The floor, their eyes closed in shame, until
They reached the cups. With their lips they tipped
The rims back so the water ran over their tongues.
Now, the master whispered, *now* look up.
They opened their eyes. They raised their heads a little.
And when they did, they saw a small oblong
Cut into the wall, and beyond that another
Cut through the hedge, and beyond that was what

They had waited for all their lives, a sight
So sublimely composed—three distant islands
Darkly shimmering on boundlessness—
That in the end they saw themselves there,
In their discomfort, in a small opening,
In a long-planned accidental moment,
In their rapture and their loss, in a view of the sea.

NOTES

THREE POEMS BY WILHELM MÜLLER

Wilhelm Müller (1794–1827) was born in Dessau, the son of a
shoemaker. He was a classicist by education and profession, and
an ardent champion of political liberty. His earliest poems were
published in 1816. His poetry is not held in high regard by literary
historians, and it is likely that, had Franz Schubert not set many of
his poems, he would be entirely, and unjustly, forgotten. In his own
day, though, his *Griechenlieder* stirred German sympathies—as
Byron roused the English—for Greece in its struggle against Turkish
rule, and Heine admired the poems Müller wrote based on his
interest in German folk song. What drew Müller was what he called
the "naturalness, truth, and simplicity" of these songs, and he strove
for just those qualities in the lyrics he wrote for two of Schubert's
great song cycles, *Die schöne Müllerin* (1824) and *Die Winterreise*
(1827). My translations are of three of *Die Winterreise*'s twenty-four
poems—"Auf dem Flusse," "Der greise Kopf," and "Der Leiermann."
The speaker is a young man, broken from a beloved, wandering
through a winter landscape both literal and emotional, toward a
death that he imagines would come as a relief. "Der Leiermann" is
the sequence's eerie last poem, and the figure of the hurdy-gurdy
man is often taken to be Death itself. All of the poems in *Die*

Winterreise, I feel, however simple their format and however familiar their tropes, emanate an uncanny power that is as moving as it is unnerving.

ONE YEAR LATER

Written to commemorate the 2011 earthquake, tsunami, and nuclear disaster in Japan.

MY ROBOTIC PROSTATECTOMY

The "three hags" referred to are the Fates of Greek mythology: Clotho, who spun the thread of an individual life; Lachesis, who measured its length; and Atropos, who cut it.

TWO ARIAS FROM *THE MARRIAGE OF FIGARO*

These two arias by Lorenzo da Ponte are highlights of Mozart's greatest opera, written in 1786. In *"Non più andrai,"* Figaro dresses the pampered, lovesick Cherubino in a uniform and sends him off to war. In *"Dove sono,"* the Countess, alone, broods on the infidelities of her husband.

HIS OWN LIFE

The italicized portions of this poem are drawn from the account by the Roman historian Tacitus of the suicide of Lucius Annaeus Seneca (4 B.C.–A.D. 65), the Stoic philosopher, writer, playwright, and tutor to the emperor Nero.

CAĞALOĞLU

The Cağaloğlu *hamam,* or public bath, in Istanbul was given to the city in 1741 by Sultan Mehmet I. It is a wonder of Ottoman architecture and has been constantly in use since it was built.

OVID'S FAREWELL

Ovid himself, in the single mysterious reference he made to the cause of his exile from Rome, spoke of *"carmen et error"*—his poem (the slyly erotic *Ars Amatoria)* and a mistake. It used to be thought that by the latter was meant he had witnessed some sexual "indiscretion" committed by Augustus's promiscuous daughter Julia—whose behavior finally led the emperor to act on his stern laws against adultery and have her banished as well. But I prefer the argument by recent historians that what Ovid had actually witnessed was a political conspiracy against the emperor of which Julia was a (perhaps unwitting) part.

Among the facts about Ovid's life we do know for certain are that he had an older brother, who died suddenly when still relatively young, and that his third and beloved wife was named Fabia. It is to her that this poem is purportedly addressed, on the night before he is to leave for the bleak, freezing penal settlement at Tomis, on the Black Sea near the mouth of the Danube, among the barbaric Getae.

The Kid (Capricorn) and the Bear (Ursa Major), Hercules and the Serpent, are constellations.

AN ESSAY ON FRIENDSHIP

Jean Renoir's film *La Règle du jeu* appeared in 1939. The two friends of mine mentioned are the sculptor Natalie Charkow Hollander and the novelist James McCourt.

TATTOOS

The first and third sections are anecdotal and symmetrical in their matching design of patterned and rhymed stanzas. The middle section is different, a discursive run of syllabics that speculates on the practice and theory of tattooing, of ornamenting the body.

The first section is set in Chicago in the late 1960s. Three raw recruits, or boots, from the Great Lakes Naval Training Center get drunk one night and end up at the local tattoo parlor—or tat shack, as it's called. Flashes are those predesigned emblems one can choose. A sleeve is a tattooed scene that covers one's entire arm, wrist to shoulder. The third sailor gets one of these, and by flexing a muscle or moving his arm, he can make the tattooed underwater scene come to a strange life. I should add that the first of the recruits has what used to be called "unspoken desires" for the second.

The third section takes place in late-nineteenth-century New Zealand. Maori chieftains used to have extraordinary facial tattoos, geometrical patterns that covered their whole heads, as a symbol of their authority. Authority has always depended on impressing one's friends and frightening one's enemies, and these tattoos were meant to do just that. In the poem, a chieftain's eldest son is having one of these tattoos cut in. Toward the end of the procedure, the pain is so great that he lapses into a delirium in which he reimagines the Maori creation myth—which holds that Father Sky and Mother Earth were once a single entity, driven apart by the sons they carried in the darkness their combined bodies had created.

SORROW IN 1944

"Sorrow" is the name Cio-Cio-San gives to her child by Benjamin Franklin Pinkerton in Puccini's opera *Madama Butterfly*. Abandoned by her lover, who with his new American wife plans to take the three-year-old child with him back to his homeland, Butterfly is preparing to commit suicide when the boy rushes to her side. She takes him in her arms and begs that he never know his mother killed herself for his sake. Before blindfolding him, she asks that he take one last look at her face so that a trace of it will remain in his memory.

The poem imagines that boy decades later, living in San Francisco and having himself fallen in love with a Japanese-American girl who has been interned in a Wyoming camp during the war. Frank— improbably described in the opera as being a blond, blue-eyed child—has escaped the fate of fellow Japanese-Americans, perhaps all the more to be haunted by a past he can only dimly recall. Dwight Eisenhower's brother Milton, as director of the War Relocation Authority, supervised the transfer of Japanese-American citizens to remote work camps. After 1942, 120,000 people of Japanese ancestry were, for alleged security reasons, forcibly removed from their homes on the West Coast. They were first taken to "assembly centers"— often fairgrounds or racing tracks—and later assigned to one of the ten relocation centers. Heart Mountain, a treeless plain between Powell and Cody, near the Shoshone Rover, eventually housed 14,000 people in hastily constructed barrack buildings, where the internees organized a school system, a newspaper and movie houses, farming crews, sports teams, and scout troops. Not until December 1944 did

the Supreme Court declare it illegal to hold American citizens in
camps against their will.

In the sequence's third and tenth sonnets, which both view the
story through the lens of Japanese legend, for the final couplet I have
substituted a rhymed tanka.

THREE OVERTURES
Each of the poem's three sections is named for a famous
overture—by, respectively, Beethoven, Mendelssohn, and Suppé.

GOING BACK TO BED
"The old pilgrim" is Dante, in *Purgatorio* XXVI.

FULL CAUSE OF WEEPING
The title is from *King Lear* II.iv.

ACKNOWLEDGMENTS

New poems in this book were first published in *The American Scholar, The New Yorker, The New York Review of Books, Ploughshares, Raritan, The Times Literary Supplement, The Warwick Review*; in *Art and Artists,* edited by Emily Fragos (Knopf, 2012); in *March Was Made of Yarn,* edited by Elmer Luke and David Karashima (Vintage, 2012); in *Crossing State Lines: An American Renga,* edited by Bob Holman and Carol Muske-Dukes (Farrar, Straus and Giroux, 2011); and in my *Seven Mozart Librettos* (Norton, 2010). Susan Bianconi, Deborah Garrison, Jeffrey Posternak, and the Knopf production team have all been stalwart friends of this book and of its grateful author.

A NOTE ABOUT THE AUTHOR

J. D. McClatchy is the author of seven collections of poetry, and of three collections of prose. He has edited numerous other books, including *The Vintage Book of Contemporary American Poetry,* and has written a number of opera libretti that have been performed at the Metropolitan Opera, Covent Garden, La Scala, and elsewhere. He is a member of the Academy of Arts and Letters, where he served as president from 2009 to 2012. McClatchy teaches at Yale University and is editor of *The Yale Review.*

A NOTE ON THE TYPE

The text of this book was set in Century Schoolbook, one of several variations of Century Roman to appear within a decade of its creation. The original Century Roman face was cut by Linn Boyd Benton (1844–1932) in 1895, in response to a request by Theodore Low De Vinne for an attractive, easy-to-read typeface to fit the narrow columns of his *Century Magazine*.

Century Schoolbook was specifically designed for school textbooks in the primary grades, but its great legibility quickly earned it popularity in a range of applications. Century remains the only American face cut before 1910 that is still widely in use today.

Composed by North Market Street Graphics, Lancaster, Pennsylvania
Printed and bound by Thomson Shore, Dexter, Michigan
Designed by Chip Kidd and Maggie Hinders